Gorgias

Bolotin, David. *Plato's Dialogue on Friendship: An Interpretation of the "Lysis," with a New Translation*

Kojève, Alexandre. *Introduction to the Reading of Hegel: Lectures on the "Phenomenology of Spirit."* Assembled by Raymond Queneau. Edited by Allan Bloom. Translated by James H. Nichols Jr.

Medieval Political Philosophy: A Sourcebook. Edited by Ralph Lerner and Muhsin Mahdi

Plato. *Gorgias.* Translated by James H. Nichols Jr.

Plato. *Phaedrus.* Translated by James H. Nichols Jr.

Plato. *Gorgias* and *Phaedrus.* Translated by James H. Nichols Jr.

The Roots of Political Philosophy: Ten Forgotten Socratic Dialogues. Edited by Thomas L. Pangle.

Rousseau, Jean-Jacques. *Politics and the Arts: Letter to M. D'Alembert on the Theatre.* Translated by Allan Bloom

PLATO
Gorgias

TRANSLATED WITH
INTRODUCTION, NOTES, AND AN
INTERPRETATIVE ESSAY BY

JAMES H. NICHOLS JR.

Cornell University Press

ITHACA AND LONDON

First published 1998 by Cornell University Press.
First printing, Cornell Paperbacks, 1998.

Printed in the United States of America.

Cornell University Press strives to use environmentally responsible suppliers and
materials to the fullest extent possible in the publishing of its books. Such materials
include vegetable-based, low-VOC inks and acid-free papers that are also recycled,
totally chlorine-free, or partly composed of nonwood fibers.

Library of Congress Cataloging-in-Publication Data

Plato
    [Gorgias. English]
    Gorgias / Plato ; translated with introduction, notes, and an
interpretive essay by James H. Nichols, Jr.
        p.   cm. — (Agora paperback editions)
    Includes bibliographical references and index.
    ISBN 0-8014-8527-4 (pbk. : alk. paper)
    1. Ethics, Ancient.   2. Political science—Early works to 1800.
I. Nichols, James H., 1944– . II. Title. III. Series.
B371.A5N53   1998
170—dc21   98-26833
                                                                    CIP

Paperback printing   10 9 8 7 6 5 4 3 2 1

Contents

Dialogue Names and Abbreviations

(Names appear spelled out at first instance and are abbreviated thereafter.)

Gorgias

Callicles	CAL.
Socrates	SOC.
Chaerophon	CHAE.
Gorgias	GOR.
Polus	POL.

Preface

The design and execution of this volume rest on three premises. First, that the questions regarding the nature of rhetoric and its proper relation to philosophy, politics, and education are of perennial concern and importance. Second, that Plato's investigation of these questions is profound and valuable for our own thinking. And third, that a careful translation by the same person of both *Gorgias* and *Phaedrus*, with notes and interpretative suggestions, could be very helpful for those wishing to come to grips with Plato's understanding of rhetoric.

Of course, I hold these premises to be true and to provide sufficient justification for the present volume. In fact, these premises seem to me sufficiently modest that I imagine most people might well agree with them. I further believe that substantially stronger assertions along each of these lines are defensible, though of necessity more controversial, and that these assertions make a far more compelling case for the value of this volume.

My full argument for these stronger assertions is to be found in the entirety of the volume that follows, including introduction, translations, notes, and suggestions for interpretation. Let me sketch them here briefly as follows.

First, rhetoric is the crucial link between philosophy and politics and must take an important place in education if political life and intellectual activity are to be in the best shape possible. While it is easy to denigrate the art of persuasion, most obviously by contrasting its possible deceptiveness with the truth of genuine knowledge, science, or philosophy, one should never forget the fundamental political fact that human beings must coordinate their activities with other human beings in order to live well, and

that the two most basic modes of such coordination are through persuasion and by force. Everyone knows the disadvantages of excessive reliance
by a political community on force or violence. If the highest intellectual
activities—science, philosophy—are to have much efficacy in practical political life, rhetoric must be the key intermediary.

Second, Plato presented the first full investigation of the most important
and fundamental questions about rhetoric, and its relation to philosophy
on the one hand and politics on the other. His investigation is classic, in the
sense that one can argue with plausibility that no later investigation has
surpassed its clarity and force on the basic questions. His understanding
of these questions and his philosophic suggestions about rhetoric deci-
sively affected the way these matters were viewed and dealt with for many
centuries and remain indispensable today.

Third, Plato's teaching on rhetoric is an aspect of his thought that is very
often misunderstood. Several features of the intellectual life of the last century or two make it difficult for many scholars to take the issue of rhetoric
as seriously as Plato himself did. Hence, for example, they are often mis-
led to think that, although the *Gorgias* does of course discuss rhetoric, it is
more deeply concerned with justice or philosophy. And similarly regarding the *Phaedrus,* many are reluctant to see rhetoric as its central theme.
New translations of both great Platonic dialogues on rhetoric, done by one
translator animated by the concern to recover a fuller and more adequate
understanding of Plato's teaching on rhetoric, may be just what the philosophical doctor ordered for those who sense the need to take a fresh and
sustained look at the problem of rhetoric.

So much for the overall design of this volume. Now a few words on particular aspects, starting with the translations. In his preface to *The Dialogues of Plato* (New Haven: Yale University Press, 1984), R. E. Allen makes
an elegant statement of a translator's need to make "the tactful adjustment
of competing demands which cannot each be fully satisfied" (xi–xii). He
discusses these demands under the names *fidelity, neutrality,* and *literalness.* My own adjustment puts considerable weight on literalness, with a
view to trying to provide the reader with as direct an access to Plato as possible and with as little dependency as possible on the translator's interpretative understanding. In the preface to *"The Republic" of Plato* (New
York: Basic Books, 1968), Allan Bloom's statement of the case against the
search for contemporaneous equivalents and in favor of a literalist tilting
of the balance is compelling—all the stronger, I find, because he criticizes
the leading nonliteral translations not by digging up some passages to

blame (which one can do to any translation) but by examining sample passages that the translators themselves singled out as exemplary of the excellence of their approach.

On the basis of my own experience, I would supplement Bloom's statement on behalf of literal translation in the following way. One could pursue the goal of being literal to whatever degree one might choose. But because words in two languages rarely correspond well in a one-to-one mapping, the more literal one wishes to be, the more notes one must add, either to explain one's word-for-word translation more fully, when necessary, so as not to mislead the reader; or where one cannot translate word for word, to point out that a particular Greek word is the same one that one has translated differently elsewhere. Too many such notes, however, would make the translation unbearable. One must therefore choose to which Greek words one will devote this close treatment and to which ones not. In the choice of where to be fully literal and to add notes, one cannot help subjecting the reader to dependence on one's interpretation.

That statement of the problem does not vitiate the goal of choosing to be literal rather than not, up to a point. It simply clarifies just why the goal of literalness can be attained only within some limits, and it suggests that the translator might well try to indicate what the principles of choice in that domain have been. The reader may of course gain fuller information on that point by looking at the actual notes to the translation itself.

Here I wish to indicate three principles by which my own choice of when to strive for literalness has been guided. First, as my opening remarks on rhetoric suggest, I pay especially close literal attention to words related to rhetoric, persuasion, speech, and the like. Second—a principle that, regrettably, I find myself able to state only vaguely—I strive for especial literalness with those words that most people concerned with philosophy, morality, and politics consider of obviously central importance (*the good, the beautiful, the just, the city, love, wisdom,* and so on). Third, any Greek expressions which, when translated literally, may sound odd but yet do not really mislead, I try to translate quite literally (oaths, terms for superhuman beings, strange vocatives, and the like).

The notes to the translation are chiefly philological and historical, rather than interpretative. I have just admitted, of course, that my philological notes explanatory to the translation rest implicitly, at least in part, on an overall interpretation; yet such notes are in themselves linguistic rather than interpretative, and I have expressed my interpretation in the introduction and in the essays on each dialogue. The historical notes aim to provide necessary or useful information, mostly noncontroversial, to facilitate understanding of the dialogues by readers who are not especially learned in ancient Greek literature or history. In addition to these two types of notes, I have pointed out certain parallels, references, or contrasts between the *Gorgias* and the *Phaedrus*.

Whole books have been written on each of these fascinating dialogues. My interpretative essays propose lines of interpretation concerning what I take to be the central theme of rhetoric. Given their brevity and the limitations of their author's own understanding, these essays are meant to be suggestive, not definitive, and I have no doubt that my readers will take them in that spirit.

In the introduction, I begin by reflecting on our present circumstances as regards rhetoric and how we got there. I introduce Plato's examination of rhetoric by arguing first that both dialogues do indeed have rhetoric as their central theme. I seek to set the stage for the more detailed study of these dialogues by presenting some preliminary thoughts on why Plato gave us two dialogues on this theme and on how these two dialogues relate to each other.

My translation of the *Gorgias* is based on the edition of E. R. Dodds, *Plato; Gorgias* (A Revised Text with Introduction and Commentary) (Oxford: Clarendon Press, 1959). I have constantly relied on his learned notes, and in my own notes all references to Dodds are to his commentary on the Greek text. Throughout I have also consulted the detailed and careful philosophical analyses of the *Gorgias* presented by Terence Irwin, *Plato; Gorgias* (Translated with Notes) (Oxford: Clarendon Press, 1979). In the fall of 1976, while I was teaching a seminar on the *Gorgias* (at the Graduate Faculty of the New School), I read the transcript (since mislaid) of a seminar given on the dialogue by Leo Strauss at the University of Chicago; I want to acknowledge my intellectual debt to that most thought-provoking seminar.

My companion translation of the *Phaedrus* is based on J. Burnet, *Platonis Opera*, Oxford Classical Texts, vol. 2 (Oxford: Clarendon Press, 1901). I have repeatedly consulted the learned notes presented by G. J. De Vries (and have often followed his readings where different from Burnet's) in his *Commentary on the "Phaedrus" of Plato* (Amsterdam: A. M. Hakkert, 1969), and in my own notes all references to De Vries are to that commentary. I have throughout also consulted the translation and notes of Léon Robin, *Platon: Oeuvres Complètes* (Greek text and French translation), Tome IV—3ᵉ Partie: *Phèdre* (Paris: Société d'Edition Les Belles Lettres, 1954).

I have frequently used the great dictionary (abbreviated in my notes as LSJ) *A Greek-English Lexicon,* by H. G. Liddell and R. S. Scott, new edition revised and augmented by H. S. Jones (Oxford: Clarendon Press, 1940 [reprinted 1961]).

I wish to acknowledge the generous assistance provided me by the Lynde and Harry Bradley Foundation, for which I am most grateful. Thanks to this assistance I was able to extend a sabbatical and take some additional leave to work on this lengthy project. I have also benefited from the sabbatical granted me by Claremont McKenna College and by a summer grant from Claremont McKenna College's Gould Center for the Humanities.

During the twenty years in which I worked with varying degrees of intensity on these dialogues of Plato, I received intellectual support, criticism, and suggestions from many friends and colleagues and benefited from much conversation with them as well as with students. Among those to whom I am grateful for discussions about Plato on many occasions are Victor Baras, Allan Bloom, David Bolotin, Christopher Bruell, Hillel Fradkin, Arthur Melzer, and Thomas Pangle. I want to acknowledge valuable comments on various parts of this work, comments that I have received from Joseph Bessette, James Ceaser, Lorraine Smith Pangle, and Paul Ulrich, and to thank Cornell University Press's anonymous reader for unusually thorough, careful, and helpful suggestions.

Without the encouragement of my wife, Merle Naomi Stern, I doubt that I should ever have completed this work. I dedicate it to her.

Gorgias

Introduction: Rhetoric, Philosophy, and Politics

In less than a century and a half, our public discourse has undergone an astonishing decline. The remarkable eloquence of leading public speakers from an earlier time finds hardly a weak echo in the present. This difference may be explained, at least in part, by the difference in political situation. Then, the greatest political issues were at stake, strife verging on civil war tore the republic apart, and political rhetoric rose to meet these challenges. Now, we enjoy stable political tranquillity, and our public speech, concerned with smaller matters, has sunk to a lower level.

So say participants in Tacitus's *Dialogue on Oratory,* who compare the public speakers of their own time with Cicero.[1] Would we not take a similar view if we should set speeches by leading political figures today next to those of Abraham Lincoln?

Now, although some speakers in Tacitus refer the decline of rhetoric to the blessings of political stability in their time, we may be sure that this cheerful thought is not the whole story for Tacitus. All his works are meditations on the causes and consequences of the loss of republican self-government. He makes it abundantly clear that his time differs from Rome's glorious past most importantly in its being ruled no longer in a republican but in a basically monarchical and sometimes tyrannical manner. That change has profound effects on political speech.

---

1. Tacitus, *Dialogue on Oratory,* sections 24 and 36. Cicero is referred to as active about 120 years before the dialogue's dramatic date.

1

Likewise today, no sensible observer could attribute the decline in our political rhetoric solely to the absence of imminent danger of civil war. We seem, to be sure, nowhere near the loss of republican government; yet we can nonetheless detect signs of substantially decreased public participation in politics, less sustained attention to and less clear understanding of political affairs, less widespread experience in political speech. Has some formerly available knowledge about rhetoric and politics slipped from our habitual grasp? Surely the reasons one might give for a decline in our political speech are all too multifarious. Perhaps everyone's favorite culprit is the rise of mass media, which appear to bring ever-shortening attention spans to the ever less thoughtful minds of the mass political audience. Each of the Lincoln-Douglas debates lasted three hours: an opening speech of one hour, followed by the second speaker's address lasting an hour and a half, and concluded with a half hour's rebuttal by the first. Our televised presidential debates are short responses to journalists' questions; and the length of the average excerpt from a presidential candidate's speech presented on national network news broadcasts in a recent election was seventeen seconds.

Crucial to the degradation of our political speech, I believe, are confusion about what rhetoric is and inattention to its necessary and proper place in politics and in education. These failures of understanding have contributed to a decline in the study and thoughtful practice of rhetoric.

Today's lack of clarity about rhetoric can be seen most evidently in the confusingly varied ways in which we use the term *rhetoric*. Rhetoric's precise nature and scope remain altogether indeterminate. In particular, popular usage and the most advanced academic usage of the term diverge sharply. *Rhetoric* in popular usage is almost always a term of disparagement. The phrase "mere rhetoric" typically designates deceptively fashioned speech whose meaning stands at odds with the speaker's real purposes. Politicians are taunted by their opponents and exhorted by political commentators to cut out the rhetoric and tell us what they would really do to deal with our problems. Many intellectuals reflect this point of view when, in treating some topic or other, they set *rhetoric* and *reality* in opposition to each other. A completely different usage occurs, however, among academics influenced by the latest academic trend, postmodernism. Such academics tend to give an immensely broad meaning to *rhetoric:* it is the study and practice of how discourse is carried on in any area whatsoever, comprehending the rules of discourse that obtain in any area as well as an account of how they came into being and continue to change. In accordance with this usage, we would have rhetorics pertaining to the whole range of subject matters from literary criticism to economics and even mathematics.[2]

In the time of Socrates, too, *rhetoric* was a much-disputed term, as we see most clearly in Plato's dialogues. Gorgias in the dialogue named for him believes that his art or science of rhetoric is the greatest of human goods and the cause of freedom for oneself and rule over others. By contrast, Socrates declares his view that what is generally called rhetoric is no art at all, but the mere knack of a certain kind of flattery. Socrates distinguishes rhetoric from sophistry but indicates that they are often confused with each other. Later in the dialogue, however, Socrates suggests the possibility of a real art of rhetoric that would serve justice and the political good. When Socrates questions Gorgias in search of just what Gorgias's rhetoric is, Socrates narrows down the definition to public persuasion of large groups and distinguishes mere persuasion of that sort from teaching the truth about things. Speaking for himself in the *Phaedrus*, by contrast, Socrates suggests a broad definition of rhetoric that would apply to individuals as well as groups and would include the teaching of genuine knowledge. What, then, is rhetoric for Plato's Socrates?

If it is correct that our own time experiences considerable confusion about what rhetoric is, we might receive especially valuable help in clarifying our thinking by studying Plato's treatment of this matter. Plato confronted a similarly complex situation, and the understanding he elaborated set the terms for reflection on rhetoric for a long time to come. The present volume seeks to facilitate rethinking of the problem of rhetoric through new translations, together with suggestions for interpretation, of Plato's two great dialogues on rhetoric.

RHETORIC THEN AND NOW

Socrates tells Phaedrus that a speech about something on which people hold differing opinions should begin with a definition. Rhetoric certainly appears to be such a subject, both now and at times in the past. It is hard to know which of the many competing definitions to choose as a basis for further discussion.

2. An impressive example of this approach is Donald McCloskey's *The Rhetoric of Economics* (Madison: University of Wisconsin Press, 1985).

Rhetoric clearly has to do with speaking well. But because people spoke well or poorly before anyone talked about an art of rhetoric, doubtless we should reserve the term *rhetoric* for a skill, art, or science of speaking well that has consciously and explicitly reflected on what makes for good and bad speaking. Within the Western tradition, such conscious reflection about speech emerged among the Greek Sophists, most notably Gorgias and Protagoras. It is not altogether clear how they conceived of their rhetorical art, for instance whether they clearly distinguished it from sophistry as a whole; in this respect their use of the term may well have something in common with the expansive postmodernist usage that I have already referred to. Indeed, postmodernists often praise sophistic rhetoric and deplore its loss of respectability from Plato's vigorous attack on it.

In the aftermath of Plato's effective critique of sophistic rhetoric and his suggestions for a philosophically guided rhetoric, however, rhetoric came to be conceived of in a way that remained stable in its essentials for most of Western history, and it is this conception of rhetoric that I wish to deal with now. Let me begin to sketch what rhetoric thus conceived is by presenting two definitions of it, definitions separated by nearly two millennia. Aristotle calls it "the power [or capacity or ability] in each [case whatsoever] of discerning the available means of persuasion."[3] By also calling rhetoric the counterpart of dialectic, Aristotle makes its scope in one way very broad; but its chief persuasive applications lead it to deal mainly with the kinds of matters dealt with by the sciences of politics and ethics. Francis Bacon speaks of rhetoric or the art of eloquence this way in the *Advancement of Learning:* "a science excellent, and excellently well laboured. For although in true value it is inferior to wisdom, as it is said by God to Moses, . . . it is eloquence that prevaileth in an active life. . . . The duty and office of rhetoric is to apply reason to imagination for the better moving of the will."[4]

However much these two definitions may differ, their agreement appears more substantial and important than their differences. Both distinguish between the substance of what one wishes to persuade (or the direction in which one wishes to move the will) and the verbal means of effecting that persuasion (or of actually moving the will). For both, rhetoric is very important in human life, especially, of course, in practical and, above all, political affairs. Without rhetorical capacity, the wise man or

3. Aristotle, *Rhetoric* 1355b. An accurate and helpfully annotated new translation is Aristotle, *On Rhetoric: A Theory of Civic Discourse,* trans. George A. Kennedy (New York: Oxford University Press, 1991).
4. Francis Bacon, *Advancement of Learning* 2.18.1–2.

man of knowledge can have no important effect in politics or in other human activities. Though its importance is great, rhetoric is lower in rank than science or wisdom itself. Rhetoric is not the whole of knowledge, nor even the whole of political skill and wisdom, as some Sophists may well have believed; yet it is neither negligible nor something whose importance one might reasonably foresee diminishing with time.

Rhetoric thus understood had an important place in higher education for centuries, one might say from the time of Aristotle to 1800 or so.[5] The rhetoric of the Greeks was learned and further developed by Roman orators and authors, most notably Cicero and Quintilian. In the medieval trivium of grammar, rhetoric, and logic, rhetoric's place was secure. Its scope was diminished in some respects, notably its primary use in political affairs, but expanded in others, for instance in the development of *ars praedictionis,* the rhetorical art of preaching sermons.[6] The recovery of the wisdom of antiquity by Renaissance humanism gave renewed dignity to rhetoric, in particular by reviving its civic function, which had been crucial for Aristotle and for ancient republicanism generally. Accordingly, Cicero was arguably the preeminent figure from classical antiquity for the writers and thinkers of the early Renaissance. With much variation in approach, basis, and emphasis, rhetoric remained important well into the eighteenth and nineteenth centuries: Adam Smith, for instance, gave lectures on rhetoric and belles lettres in addition to his better-known teachings on moral philosophy, jurisprudence, and political economy.[7]

Why then did rhetoric subsequently fall into eclipse? One cause was a certain way of thinking about Enlightenment. Although Francis Bacon, among the greatest founders of the Enlightenment movement, held a high view of the importance of rhetoric, Thomas Hobbes in the very next generation took a dim view of it, and John Locke a still dimmer one soon after. Hear John Locke:

> If we would speak of Things as they are, we must allow, that all the Art of
> Rhetorick, besides Order and Clearness, all the artificial and figurative ap-

---

5. So Thomas Cole puts it in his *Origins of Rhetoric in Ancient Greece* (Baltimore: Johns Hopkins University Press, 1991), p. 22.
6. On rhetoric in the Middle Ages, Murphy's introduction is helpful, in James J. Murphy, ed. *Three Medieval Rhetorical Arts* (Berkeley: University of California Press, 1971).
7. A good overall history is George A. Kennedy, *Classical Rhetoric and Its Christian and Secular Tradition from Ancient to Modern Times* (Chapel Hill: University of North Carolina Press, 1980).

plication of Words Eloquence hath invented, are for nothing else but to in-
sinuate wrong *Ideas,* move the Passions, and thereby mislead the Judgment; and so indeed are perfect cheat. . . . 'Tis evident how much Men love
to deceive, and be deceived, since Rhetorick, that powerful instrument of
Error and Deceit, has its established Professors, is publickly taught, and has
always been had in great Reputation.[8]

Rhetoric's power of deception has been an issue from the start, but it
looks especially questionable from an Enlightenment point of view. Let me
put the central idea of Enlightenment this way: the progress of knowledge,
philosophy, and science naturally harmonizes, in the long run, with the
overall well-being of political community as a whole. Most of us to this
day remain heirs of the Enlightenment to such an extent that we are in-
clined to accept that idea without much ado, but it bears emphasizing that
it is a relatively new view. Plato, for instance, did not share it. His most famous image of political society is the cave, whose members live not in the
light of the truth but with shared perceptions of shadows of man-made
artifacts.[9] The good functioning of society depends on consensus, shared
judgments, common sentiments, and the like. Philosophy disrupts all these,
of necessity, through its critical testing of mere opinion in search for genuine truths. Does the philosopher attain the truth he seeks? One cannot
confidently answer yes; Socrates, who appears in Plato's writings as the
very model of the seeker after truth, never claims to possess wisdom or
knowledge about the most important matters. If a philosopher did attain
the comprehensive or highest truth—or even truth about many of the most
important things—could truth be directly applied to make society simply
rational, or even just to improve it overall? The answer to this question is
no less uncertain. Given these two levels of uncertainties, it seems reasonable to suppose that a philosopher would always need rhetoric if he is to
be able to have any beneficial political effect at all; indeed he would need
rhetoric even for the mere presentation of his philosophical views in a politically responsible and defensible manner.

By contrast, in an Enlightenment perspective, our hopes are oriented toward the spread of real and solid knowledge. Rhetoric may be needed
now, but it should become less necessary the more progress we make. Jefferson, himself a gifted rhetorician, expresses these Enlightenment hopes

8. John Locke, *An Essay concerning Human Understanding,* bk. 3, chap. 10, sec. 34.
9. Plato, *The Republic* 7.514a–521c.

in 1826, when he writes of the fateful decision and declaration of a half-century before:

> May it be to the world, what I believe it will be (to some parts sooner, to others later, but finally to all), the signal of arousing men to burst the chains under which monkish ignorance and superstition had persuaded them to bind themselves, and to assume the blessings and security of self-government. . . . All eyes are opened, or opening, to the rights of man. The general spread of the light of science has already laid open to every view the palpable truth, that the mass of mankind has not been born with saddles on their backs, nor a favored few booted and spurred, ready to ride them legitimately, by the grace of God. These are grounds of hope for others.[10]

With the bright light of science thus ever more broadly diffused, what need for rhetoric? Surely, one seems justified to hope, a diminishing one. In the long run, the deceitful appeals and devious wiles of rhetoric will be more obstacle than help in the course of human progress.

A second, later intellectual force that drove rhetoric from its former place in education and intellectual life was the Romantic conception of Art. Indeed, this strand of thinking is more deeply opposed to the traditional conception and place of rhetoric than the Enlightenment view, and we remain, I believe, at least as much under its sway as under the other's. This conception of Art, emerging in critical reaction to certain features of the Enlightenment's worldview, holds that the highest achievements of the human spirit are the creative productions of the unique individual.[11]

---

10. Thomas Jefferson, *Selected Writings*, ed. Harvey C. Mansfield Jr. (Arlington Heights, Ill.: AHM Publishing, 1979), p. 12.

11. Let me cite three scholars who state this basic view from widely different perspectives. Brian Vickers, speaking of why it is hard for us to grasp rhetoric's past importance, states that "a prolonged effort of the historical imagination is necessary. We have to overcome . . . the distrust and opposition to rhetoric that have prevailed in European poetics and aesthetics since the post-Romantic generation" (Brian Vickers, ed., *Rhetoric Revalued: Papers from the International Society for the History of Rhetoric*, [Binghampton, N.Y.: Center for Medieval & Renaissance Studies, 1982], p. 13). Leo Strauss, speaking of the eclipse in the reputations of Xenophon, Livy, and Cicero, writes that it "has been due to a decline in the understanding of the significance of rhetoric: both the peculiar 'idealism' and the peculiar 'realism' of the 19th century were guided by the modern conception of 'Art' and for that reason were unable to understand the crucial significance of the lowly art of rhetoric" (Leo Strauss, *On Tyranny*, [New York: Free Press, 1963], p. 26). Thomas Cole refers to the "decline of the discipline in the past two centuries," which he connects to "the widely held romantic or 'expressionist' notion of the literary work as a unique or maximally adequate verbalization of a unique vision or unique individual sensibility" (*Origins of Rhetoric*, p. 19).

Let me elaborate on the ground and character of this notion by considering how it might originate from an aspect of Rousseau's thought. He makes clear that the real world as illuminated by Enlightenment philosophy and modern science has nothing in it that can satisfy our specifically human needs, concerns, passions. The human being itself, as merely natural, is subhuman, without speech, reason, society, and the arts. The natural world, as matter in motion, has no inherent beauty or appeal to our full humanity: "The existence of finite beings is so poor and so limited that when we only see what is, we are never moved. It is chimeras that adorn real objects, and if the imagination does not add a charm to what strikes us, the sterile pleasure that one takes in it is limited to the organ and always leaves the heart cold."[12] Beauty is created for us by our imagination, cultivated and developed as we move away from nature. So too, that most powerful and distinctively human passion of love is "chimera, lie, illusion. One loves much more the image that one makes for oneself than the object to which one applies it. If one saw what one loves exactly as it is, there would be no more love on earth."[13] The greatest human achievements are those of the unique genius—poet, artist, musician, and (possibly) prophet or lawgiver—whose greatness is measured by the integrity of vision and its capacity to enrich the lives of others, even whole peoples or civilizations. Only through being molded by the formative influence on their imaginations of such unique visions can people come to participate in full humanity. Not knowledge of nature, nor art as imitation of nature, but artistic creation represents the peak of humanity.

From this point of view regarding what is of the highest human worth, rhetoric is lowly indeed. Its consciously manipulative aspect is not just something different from artistic creation, but flagrantly contradicts the whole spirit of attaining and expressing one's individual vision. The self-conscious and calculated working out of the best way persuasively to state one's purpose stands diametrically opposed to authentic artistic creativity. As Keats said, "Poetry should come as naturally as the leaves to a tree: otherwise it had better not come at all."[14] Rousseau himself does not take this view; like Bacon, he greatly appreciates the classic tradition of rhetoric. But later modern trends, in losing the close touch that Rousseau still main-

---

12. Rousseau, *Oeuvres Complètes*, ed. Bernard Gagnebin and Marcel Raymond (Paris: Gallimard, Bibliothèque de la Pléiade, 1959–1969), 4:418.
13. Rousseau, *Oeuvres Complètes*, 4:656.
14. Keats, letter to John Taylor, 27 February 1818, cited by Ian Thomson, "Rhetoric and the Passions, 1760–1800," in Vickers, ed., *Rhetoric Revalued*, p. 146.

tained with classical thought and its deeply political concerns, develop this modern notion of Art in a way that leaves rhetoric as something quite contemptible: manipulative, basely calculating, falsely separating form from content, concerned with low utility, and of course deceptive.

As if the Enlightenment view of the progressive diffusion of knowledge and the Romantic view of Art were not enemies enough for the older tradition of rhetoric, democratic egalitarianism directs yet another objection to it, an old one with a new wrinkle. Although rhetoric seems naturally to flourish best in republics, democracy nonetheless has a certain hostility toward it. Because democracy rests on a kind of assumption that all are equal in the most important political respect, why should rhetoric be needed? It does not appear to be a specialized expertise, like medicine, to which it is sensible for all nonexperts to defer. If it does accomplish something, does it not thereby disrupt democratic equality, by helping the few, those with sufficient leisure and money to study rhetoric, to prevail over the many?

This problem of rhetoric's elitism, like the issue of deception, has been around from the start. Plato deals with it as we shall see in the *Gorgias* and delicately touches on it in the *Protagoras*, where Socrates compels that famous Sophist to come to terms with the problematic relation of sophistry to democracy. The problem perseveres in modern democracy, reinforced by a relativism about good and bad, noble and base things, which Plato himself had already diagnosed as an endemic tendency of democratic thinking and character. The democratic man, Socrates argues, "doesn't admit true speech . . . , if someone says that there are some pleasures belonging to fine and good desires and some belonging to bad desires, and that the ones must be practiced and honored and the others checked and enslaved. Rather, he shakes his head at all this and says that all are alike and must be honored on an equal basis."[15] The peculiar feature of our situation is that that view, in several more elaborated versions, has come to prevail in the most advanced intellectual circles. Consequently, the traditional defense of rhetoric as necessary to link wisdom to the level of understanding of the many tends to be angrily or derisively rejected as elitist, without a serious hearing. Our late modern or postmodernist sophistication is supposed to have taught us that no sweeping claims of superior knowledge regarding values can be accepted, or even examined seriously.

And yet today the discussion of rhetoric is going on full tilt, to such a degree that one can properly speak of a sharp revival of interest in rhetoric.

15. Plato, *Republic* 8.561b–c.

The most easily available evidence of this trend can be discovered through inspecting the growing number of book titles that mention rhetoric. Scholarly articles that analyze rhetoric or rhetorical aspects in literature, philosophy, and political theory likewise abound. How can this be? The key to understanding this development, I believe, is to be found in the hugely expanded sense of the term *rhetoric* that has emerged under the influence of postmodernism. Along lines drawn by Nietzsche and plowed more deeply by Heidegger, postmodernism continues the project of uprooting the Western philosophical tradition. That tradition's search for metaphysical foundations; its impulse toward what is permanent and universal rather than transient and local; its dichotomies of belief and knowledge, subject and object, truth and opinion, appearance and reality, science and rhetoric—all these ways of thinking, it is asserted, have proven to be dead ends, habits that our riper experience and reflection should lead us to outgrow. Mode of presentation, therefore, cannot be tenably distinguished from the substance of what is intended; form cannot be separated usefully from content; rhetoric cannot be soundly differentiated from science or philosophy or political goal. All discourse is rhetorical.

Now, this new way of talking about rhetoric is surely thought-provoking, doubtless contains elements of truth, and, in my judgment, may have the intellectually salutary effect of discrediting overly narrow methodologies, especially in the social sciences.[16] Yet I must wonder whether a term used so broadly as *rhetoric* is now used does not lose its usefulness for clarifying our thinking. I must wonder, too, whether we do not still need to make the distinctions that used to be made with the former meaning of the term *rhetoric*. Let us grant that many dichotomies can be misleading or narrowing if taken in a rigid or dogmatic manner. But must one not worry on the other side about unintended effects that may emerge if we reject useful, commonsensical, perhaps indispensable distinctions in our thinking? However much we may need critically to call into question the adequacy of our understanding of, say, our desire to discover permanent truths, is our thought really deepened or, on the contrary, is it rendered more superficial by dismissing such terms as obsolete relics of exploded metaphysics? After all, did not human beings display concern for truth as distinguished from hearsay or falsehood long before Plato or anyone else laid down the supposedly metaphysical foundations of Western thinking?

Postmodernist approaches in philosophy and politics seem to me at their most useful in bringing to light and criticizing distinctive features of

16. McCloskey's work in economics seems especially valuable in this regard; see note 2.

various leading traditions of modern thought (taking *modern* to mean dating from Bacon or Descartes or thereabouts). But similar critiques addressed to ancient thought appear to me far less revealing, because they seem often to rest for the most part on simplistic readings of ancient authors. This defect is most glaring as regards Plato. The eagerness to reject his allegedly rigid or absolutist dichotomies leads critics often to take tentative suggestions in Platonic dialogues for declared and settled doctrine; to ignore the significance of the context in which speakers make assertions in the dialogues; to pass over the professions of uncertainty with which assertions are framed (or to note them dismissively as mere Socratic window dressing used by the dogmatic Plato).

In fine, the postmodernist style of rejecting allegedly Platonic doctrines typically rests on simplistic accounts of what Plato is supposed to have held; especially so as regards rhetoric. Cicero's Crassus says that, in carefully reading the *Gorgias,* he admired Plato most in that "he himself seemed to me to be the supreme orator in ridiculing the orators."[17] Should not this intelligent observation motivate us to interpret Plato's critique of rhetoric with some nuance, subtlety, and irony? But instead, all too often we find Plato described simply as the bitter enemy of rhetoric.[18]

But if rhetoric should be as important as I have suggested, or as many writers today seem to think, or as most of the Western intellectual tradition appears to have held, surely it is worthwhile to look closely, with sympathetic attention, at how Plato investigated the problem of rhetoric in relation to philosophy and politics.

PRELIMINARY SKETCH OF RHETORIC'S IMPORTANCE FOR PLATO:
The Apology of Socrates AND *The Republic*

For rhetoric, as for many another important theme in Plato, *The Apology of Socrates* provides a most helpful beginning point for reflection. The *Apology* or defense speech begins with Socrates' statements on the problem of rhetoric. People skilled in rhetoric are often described as terribly clever at speaking, and Socrates' accusers have so characterized him in their speech

17. Cicero, *De Oratore* 1.47
18. For instance: Brian Vickers, *In Defence of Rhetoric* (Oxford: Clarendon Press, 1988). This book provides a valuable discussion and defense of rhetoric throughout history; but its interpretation of Plato's views of rhetoric is its weakest spot, wherein Vickers lets himself go into indignant exclamations about Plato's unfairness to Gorgias. George Kennedy's mostly excellent *Art of Persuasion in Ancient Greece* (Princeton: Princeton University Press, 1963), p. 14, likewise refers too simply to Gorgias as "the butt of [Plato's] invective against rhetoric."

before the Athenian judicial body of some five hundred citizens. Socrates denies this charge; indeed he describes it as his accusers' most shameless accusation, because they will be immediately refuted in deed by Socrates' own defense speech. But as with so many Socratic statements, this one has its complexities. Not only does this beginning of his speech exemplify some sound rhetorical technique (aiming at presenting one's character in such a way as to dispose one's hearers favorably), but Socrates himself qualifies his own disclaimer, at least hypothetically: if the accusers call terribly clever him who says true things, then Socrates agrees that he is a rhetor, though not after their manner.[19]

Socrates denies that he uses the sort of verbal devices that are usually thought to constitute rhetorically artful speech. Instead, he urges the five hundred judges to overlook his manner of speaking and to consider only whether he says just things or not; for this, he asserts, is the virtue of a judge; the virtue of a rhetor is to say true things. Thus, in his only address to the political multitude of Athens of which we have record, Socrates starts with a reflection on rhetoric and truth and emphatically draws attention to his unusual, almost foreign, views on these matters.[20]

Several times in the course of his defense speech, Socrates comments on what makes persuasion difficult in his circumstances. Despite his facing a capital charge, he must deal in but a short time with deeply rooted, because ancient, slanders. The character of Athenian political and especially judicial practices leads the jurors to expect improper things from a defendant. Socrates offers what is perhaps his most revealing comment on persuading the jurors when he has been found guilty and must propose an alternative punishment to the death sentence demanded by the prosecution. He reflects on how difficult it is to persuade them that he must carry on his present way of life unchanged. If he says that to do otherwise would be to disobey the god, "you will not be persuaded by me, on the grounds that I am being ironical." But if he asserts that his philosophic life is the greatest good for a human being and that the unexamined life is not worth living, "you will be even less persuaded by me as I say these things. But they are so, as I assert, men, but it is not easy to persuade."[21]

19. Plato, *The Apology of Socrates* 17b.
20. Plato, *Apology* 17d–18a. We know from *Apology* 32a–c that Socrates spoke to the democratic assembly in support of the lawful way of proceeding in the matter of the admirals after the battle of Arginusae; Socrates' arguments did not, however, prevail over the rhetors on that occasion either.
21. Plato, *Apology* 38a.

The *Apology* dramatizes unforgettably the most urgent, and perhaps the central, problem of political philosophy: the tension between the philosopher and the city. Socrates fails at political persuasion; the truth is politically inefficacious and unacceptable.[22] The *Apology* displays in deed what Socrates predicts in the *Gorgias* (521c–522c): that his dialectical mode of speaking with one person at a time cannot work with the many; that if accused before a multitude, he would be left gaping, with nothing to say. He would be like a doctor, administrator of surgery, cautery, bitter drugs, and harsh diets, accused by a pastry chef before a jury of children. Yet we see in the *Apology* that Socrates was willing to make *some* effort to persuade the judges: in his main defense speech he did, after all, present the more popularly persuasive account of his life as a divine mission; he did not simply develop arguments to show how his way of life is in truth the greatest human good. And he plainly asserts to those who condemned him to death that he could have found the arguments by which to get himself acquitted. What caused his condemnation was not being at a loss for speeches. It was his unwillingness to say and to do all things (including shameful things), his judgment that one ought not use all devices to avoid death, in battle or in courtroom, that led to his condemnation.[23]

If we held political rhetoric to be the capacity to persuade a political multitude to acquit one of a charge, we should have to say that Socrates possessed that rhetorical capacity but chose not to use it. Socrates is not quite the foreigner to political rhetoric that he seemed at first.

If the *Republic* is the true *apologia* of Socrates before the city,[24] one would expect to find there too some crucial reflections on rhetoric, philosophy, and politics; and the *Republic* does not disappoint in this regard. For one thing, the overall direction of discussion is set by the rhetorician Thrasymachus's contribution. It is his debunking of justice as mere convention and his praise of successful injustice that provoke Socrates to a prolonged defense of justice; thus we see the familiar and conventional picture of Socrates fighting against the rhetoricians or the sophists. And yet, at about midpoint in the discussion, Socrates asserts that he and Thrasymachus

22. Thinkers of the Enlightenment sought to overcome this tension by making truth politically efficacious and by reforming political society in accordance with reason's prescriptions. By now, however, most political scientists recognize that that hopeful endeavor has met with but partial success, at most.
23. Plato, *Apology* 38d–39a.
24. As Allan Bloom has argued persuasively in *"The Republic" of Plato* (New York: Basic Books, 1968), p. 307.

"have just become friends, though we weren't even enemies before."[25] How are we to understand this remarkable utterance? Its significance, I believe, lies in the context: Socrates' account of the philosopher rulers has made clear the crucial need for persuasion if the best city is to become a reality. He has recently exhorted Adeimantus to "teach the image [of the philosopher on the ship of the city] to that man who wonders at the philosophers' not being honored in the cities, and try to *persuade* him that it would be far more to be wondered at if they were honored."[26] He has exonerated private sophists from blame for corrupting young men, asserting instead that not any private person but the political multitude is the biggest sophist.[27] And he is about to temper Adeimantus's contempt (perhaps mixed with fear) of the opinions of the many by saying to him: "Don't make such a severe accusation against the many. They will no doubt have another sort of opinion, if instead of indulging yourself in quarreling with them, you soothe them and do away with the slander against the love of learning by pointing out whom you mean by the philosophers. . . ."[28] In the *Phaedrus* (267c–d) Socrates refers to Thrasymachus's special capacity to arouse or soothe angry passion and to slander or to dissipate slanders: within this context of the *Republic*, then, Socrates is sketching a crucial task that calls for the capacities precisely of Thrasymachus. Socrates concludes this segment of discussion by speaking as follows of those who his interlocutor had supposed would be angry at the notion that philosophers should rule: "'If you please,' I said, 'let's not say that they are less angry but that they have become in every way gentle and have been persuaded, so that from shame, if nothing else, they will agree.' 'Most certainly,' he said. 'Now, let's assume they have been persuaded of this,' I said."[29]

At this point in the *Republic*, then, Socrates appears to attribute very great power to the capacity to persuade. But is this the whole story, and his final judgment, on the power of rhetoric? To the contrary, one must remember the crucial introductory scene of the dialogue, which provided an urbane, comical representation of the twofold character of politics as consisting of both persuasion and force. To Polemarchus's proposition that Socrates and Glaucon must either prove stronger than his group or else

25. Plato, *Republic* 6.498c–d. This friendship does not prevent Socrates from once again making clear that Thrasymachus praises injustice and hence tyranny (8.545a).
26. Plato, *Republic* 6.489a, emphasis added.
27. Plato, *Republic* 6.492a–b.
28. Plato, *Republic* 6.499e.
29. Plato, *Republic* 6.501e–502a.

stay in the Piraeus, Socrates suggested the alternative possibility of "our persuading you that you must let us go." But, Polemarchus asked, "Could you really persuade, if we don't listen?"[30] Surely Plato thus reminds us of the ever-present limitations on the power of rhetoric. Accordingly, although education in the *Republic* as a whole does indeed use rhetorical persuasion, it also works through habituation from a very early age, laws with penalties, and even deceptive uses of authoritative divine ceremonies like sacred lotteries. Rhetoric may be powerful but it is surely not all-powerful.

RHETORIC AS THE CENTRAL THEME OF THE *Gorgias* AND *Phaedrus*

Just how powerful is rhetoric? That is the question in Socrates' mind when he goes with his friend Chaerephon to the place where the famous rhetorician Gorgias has been displaying his art. In explaining his desire to converse with Gorgias, Socrates tells Callicles that he wants to learn "what the power of the man's art is, and what it is that he professes and teaches" (447c).

The interlocutors in the *Gorgias* deal with the most important questions—such great matters as whether justice or injustice is superior, and whether the philosophic life or the life of political action is best for a human being. What is more, Socrates speaks about these things with a degree of passionate engagement that many a reader finds deeply moving. For these reasons, many commentators reject the view that the dialogue is chiefly about rhetoric. They prefer to take the investigation of rhetoric as merely the occasion for a discussion that moves on to weightier philosophic and moral questions.[31] Without in any way denying that loftier subjects are indeed discussed in the dialogue at considerable length, I nonetheless wish to maintain that what ties the dialogue into a whole and makes sense of its several parts is indeed what Socrates had in mind from the start, namely the question of rhetoric and its power. In this place I shall briefly state four lines of argument, which I elaborate in more detail in the interpretative essay on the *Gorgias*.

First, then, the dialogue is named for the rhetorician Gorgias, even though he speaks a good deal less than, for instance, Callicles. Could this

30. Plato, *Republic* 1.327c.
31. Brian Vickers for example follows many others in saying that the "real subject" of the dialogue is "the rival claims of politics and philosophy to represent the good life" (*In Defence of Rhetoric*, p. 103).

not be because Gorgias is the most famous interlocutor? To be sure, but Plato does not always assign names in that manner: the dialogue on courage, for instance, is named the *Laches* not the *Nicias*. Furthermore, Gorgias's intervention is crucial for the dialogue's being carried through to a conclusion instead of breaking off unfinished. These facts suggest a close relation between the dialogue's theme and the rhetorician Gorgias.

Second, Socrates permits or rather compels the conversation to move from rhetoric to questions of justice and the best human life; yet on each occasion he makes the effort to bring it back to the subject of rhetoric—most notably, even in the closing myth about the soul's fate after death.

Third, near the beginning of the discussion (448d–e), Socrates distinguishes rhetoric from dialectic or conversation. He characterizes Polus's first speech about Gorgias's art as rhetorical, because it failed to say *what* the art is and instead said *what kind of* thing it is and praised it as if it had been attacked. Dialectic, we are left to presume, answers the question *what a thing is*. But when Socrates later overturns Polus's assertion that doing injustice without paying a just penalty is better than suffering injustice, the whole refutation turns on the premise granted by Polus (474c) that doing injustice is baser than suffering injustice; it rests, in other words, on an assertion of *what kind of* thing injustice is without making clear *what* it is. At this crucial point of the discussion, then, Socrates refutes rhetorically rather than investigates dialectically. May we not infer that Socrates is concerned with rhetoric to an exceptional degree in this dialogue?

Fourth, in his discussion with Callicles, Socrates is more openly self-conscious about persuasion, more explicitly concerned with his success or failure at persuading his interlocutor, than in any other dialogue, except perhaps the *Apology*. For instance, in driving Callicles from his position of immoderate hedonism (492d–499b), Socrates first evokes strange myths that confound life and death and compare the soul to a perforated jar. "Well, am I *persuading* you somewhat and do you change over to the position that the orderly are happier than the intemperate?" Socrates asks. When Callicles denies it, Socrates uses another likeness, of two sets of jars, and then again asks, "Do I somewhat *persuade* you . . . or do I not *persuade* you?" Next, Socrates tries to shame Callicles into abandoning his position by arguments about inflows and outpourings and the like. Callicles tells Socrates he should be ashamed of himself, Socrates returns the charge, but Callicles maintains his position. Socrates next tries an argument to show how our way of experiencing pain and pleasure differs from our experiencing of clearly good and bad things like health and sickness. Here Callicles becomes decidedly recalcitrant: he denies that he understands Socrates' "sophisms" and belittles

Socrates' kinds of questions and examples; he continues only in consequence of Gorgias's effective urging. When Socrates has completed *that* argument, he presents another, "for," he says, "I think it is not agreed on by
you in this way." This other argument *does* finally lead Callicles to abandon
immoderate hedonism, if with ill grace. The previous argument failed, it
seems, because of its rather abstract, theoretical character. The last one
works by linking the issue of the good and the pleasant to something that
Callicles cares deeply about: the prudence and courage of the superior men.

What are we to make of these multiple attempts at persuasion? Socrates,
it seems to me, experiments with, or demonstrates before Gorgias, various
modes of persuasion. Socrates starts with what he does least well and ends
with the dialectic that he is best at. Or one could say, he starts with the
mode that could work best with large numbers of people and ends with
what can work best with a given individual. For Gorgias, perhaps, the re-
verse order would hold: he could do best at elaborating the tales and images that Socrates presents flatly and ineffectively. Thus, I suggest, a possible division of persuasive labor between philosopher and rhetorician is
provisionally sketched. Whatever merit that suggestion may have, the emphasis on persuasion and the concern with rhetoric clearly appear central
to Socrates' proceedings.

When we turn to the *Phaedrus*, it is yet more problematic to determine
the central theme. Indeed, the very being of the *Phaedrus* itself, as a written
text, is perhaps the most striking irony in Plato's writings. We behold Socrates, who left behind no writing, denigrating the value of writing as such
and arguing that a serious man can only regard his writings as playful
side-occupations—and this we read written by Plato, in whom virtually
every serious reader discerns a most careful and polished writer. We learn
that a writing should have a unity like that of a living being, with all its
parts suitably adapted to the whole; yet the unity of the *Phaedrus* is as hard
to articulate as that of any dialogue in the whole Platonic corpus.

The central difficulty here, of course, is to understand just what kind of
whole is constituted by the *Phaedrus*'s two main parts: speeches about
love, and discussions of speech writing and rhetoric. Some ancient editor
gave the *Phaedrus* the subtitle "On Love"; other ancient scholars, however,
maintained that its chief subject was rhetoric. Hermias affirmed that it was
"about the beautiful of all kinds."[32] A thoughtful and thorough recent book
on the *Phaedrus* argues that the question of self-knowledge provides the

32. Hermias, cited in G. J. De Vries, *A Commentary on the "Phaedrus" of Plato* (Amsterdam:
A. M. Hakkert, 1969), p. 22.

central and unifying theme.[33] In my own view, the recent commentator De Vries puts it about right. He asserts that rhetoric, or "the persuasive use of words," is the central theme, with beauty, knowledge, and love treated as topics intertwined with the inquiry into the foundations of persuasion.[34] In what follows, I try to lend further support to this position by showing how the *Phaedrus* and *Gorgias* complement each other so as to present Plato's full understanding of rhetoric.

THE TWOFOLD CHARACTER OF PLATO'S TREATMENT OF RHETORIC

I can state the gist of my view of the relation of Plato's two treatments of rhetoric in the form of a proportion: as the *Republic* is to the *Symposium,* so is the *Gorgias* to the *Phaedrus;* or equivalently, the *Gorgias* stands in relation to the *Republic* as the *Phaedrus* does to the *Symposium.* To restate this point in terms of central themes: the *Republic* deals with justice, the *Symposium* with *erōs* or love; the *Gorgias* treats rhetoric about justice, the *Phaedrus* rhetoric about love.

Before elaborating this point in regard to the different presentations of rhetoric in the *Gorgias* and *Phaedrus,* I need to sketch one general reflection on the character of each Platonic dialogue and on the relations between them, which I shall illustrate with a comment on the relation of the *Republic* to the *Symposium.* Each of Plato's many dialogues is decidedly one-sided or partial. It pursues a particular approach to an issue, or a limited aspect of an issue, or a special point of view on an issue; or it treats an issue with a view to meeting some particular human need in the circumstances; or in some other way it is particular, partial, limited in its scope. In consequence, if one is to understand Plato's thought fully, one needs to supplement what one sees in any single dialogue with what can be learned from other dialogues. Doubtless, complete understanding of Plato's thinking would require full knowledge of every dialogue and adequate reflection on their interrelations. Yet even if such knowledge is unavailable to us, one may nevertheless sensibly observe that in studying a given dialogue on one particular theme, one can often see some rather obvious reasons why another one or two or three dialogues are especially necessary to supplement the partiality of the given one.

33. Charles L. Griswold Jr., *Self-Knowledge in Plato's "Phaedrus"* (New Haven : Yale University Press, 1986.)
34. De Vries, *Commentary on the "Phaedrus,"* p. 23.

For example, in dealing with perfect justice and the best city, the *Republic* downplays, abstracts from, and rides roughshod over *erōs*.[35] In particular, the argument builds on an inadequately supported, at best provisional, assertion that spiritedness is superior to desire of all kinds, including erotic desire. Consequently, for understanding more fully this crucial dimension of the human soul, or of human nature, one is most emphatically directed toward the *Symposium* as the necessary supplement.

In spite of what I have just said, each dialogue by itself is a complete and complex whole; each dialogue's chief thrust and emphasis may be one-sided, but each does at least allude to what it mainly passes over or distorts. Thus even if we had no *Symposium* to read, we could (though with more difficulty and without the help of as full a treatment by Plato) at least discern from a careful reading of the *Republic* that the very *erōs* being by and large crushed for the sake of the perfect city does nonetheless have its higher aspects. Socrates does make clear, after all, that not only the tyrant but also the philosopher is defined by his *erōs*. He makes perfectly clear, too, that even the austere education of the guardians culminates in *erōs* of the beautiful.

With these general considerations in mind, let us consider how rhetoric is treated in the two dialogues. The *Gorgias*, within the context of its treatment of rhetoric, resembles the *Republic* in some crucial ways, most notably its downplaying of *erōs*. The *Gorgias* presents rhetoric as, almost by definition, addressed to many people in some kind of political gathering. Socrates contrasts rhetoric starkly with dialectic, the one-on-one conversational mode of proof that he practices. He emphatically states that he does not converse with the many. In fact, he presents himself overall as if quite ignorant of what rhetoric is and what it can do. For most of the discussion, Socrates pursues the inquiry in such a way as to narrow the subject matter with which rhetoric is concerned down to justice. He attacks existing rhetoric chiefly on the grounds of justice: rhetoric pursues pleasure through flattery rather than genuine good through justice. And he presents justice itself largely as the art of correct punishing by the constituted political/judicial authority, whereby the soul of the unjust man is cured of its illness. The principal cause of injustice comes to sight as immoderate, unchastened desires, so that the health of soul at which just punishment aims seems to be most clearly denominated as moderation or even austerity. The discussion emphasizes the harshness and the pain connected with just

35. Leo Strauss, *The City and Man* (Chicago: Rand McNally, 1964), p. 111.

punishment. The closing myth presents gods who judge and punish souls after death; in keeping with the earlier emphases, here too the vivid details chiefly involve painful punishments.

Although during much of the *Gorgias* Socrates attacks most rhetoric as flattery without genuine art, he nonetheless points toward the possibility of a true rhetoric, or a true political art, that would strive to make citizens more just and better. In criticizing actual statesmen like Pericles for lacking this art, Socrates uses the unstated premise that such an art would be all-powerful. But when he himself claims to be the only person who practices the true political art, Socrates admits that he has no political rhetorical effectiveness or political power in the usual sense, thus suggesting that this true political art is altogether without power. We are left to infer that a true rhetorical art devoted to promoting justice could have a measure of power lying somewhere between the extremes of all or nothing.

How sharply the *Phaedrus* contrasts with the *Gorgias*! At least as sharply, I venture to say, as the *Symposium* contrasts with the *Republic.* The dialogue takes place between two people outside the city walls, in contrast to the large gathering before whom Socrates converses with Gorgias and others. The *Phaedrus*'s discussion of rhetoric arises in connection with speeches about *erōs;* the substantive matters discussed are largely private, with only brief[36] references to anything political. Although of course never blaming moderation or sobriety, Socrates nonetheless presents a remarkable praise of *erōs* as a kind of divine madness. Socrates here is so far from rejecting long speeches, as he ostentatiously does in the *Gorgias,* that he describes himself as sick with desire for speeches and delivers one much longer than any in the *Gorgias.* Socrates shows himself to be very well informed about contemporary rhetoric. He criticizes that rhetoric not on the grounds of justice and politics, but for inadequately artful or scientific procedures. He does not explicitly discuss the question of rhetoric's power, but his own remarks on developing a proper art of rhetoric would seem to aim at, among other things, making it more reliably effective. When he develops his own notion of rhetoric, he does not limit it to political rhetoric, but suggests a universal art of *psychagōgia*, the leading of souls. The real art of rhetoric would not be something to be sharply contrasted with dialectic, but would

36. But not necessarily for that reason unimportant; the reference to lawgivers like Solon as writers, for instance, surely provides significant matter for reflection on what Socratic or Platonic rhetoric might aim at. Rhetoric combines with compulsory legislation in a noteworthy manner through the Athenian Stranger's proposal for persuasive preludes to laws (*Laws* 722d–724a).

need to be developed by a person skilled in dialectic, who made, concerning human souls and their actions and passions, all the synoptic definitions and the analytical divisions in accordance with the natural articulations of things necessary to develop a true rhetorical science. And certainly the philosopher would have a definite leg up on performing this work. The gods are no less present in the *Phaedrus* than in the *Gorgias,* indeed they are more so, but here they come to sight as objects of our *erōs* or rather as leaders of our endeavor to behold the truly beautiful.

How can two such disparate treatments be put together into a coherent whole that we may call Plato's understanding of rhetoric? Overall, the more closely one examines assertions made in each dialogue, with due regard to context and to various stated or implicit qualifications, the more one finds them to be not so much contradictory as complementary. To give one important example: rhetoric in the *Gorgias* comes to sight chiefly as political, which is taken to mean directed above all or even exclusively to the many. Because the most common source of political ills is immoderate desires, good rhetoric according to the *Gorgias* seeks above all to create order, geometrical proportion, harmony, and restraint in the souls of citizens; these traits are favored by the gods, who endorse human punitive justice and perfect it after death. The *Phaedrus,* on the other hand, deals chiefly with the few who especially give thought to speeches, among whom might be found those who could develop a true art of rhetoric. Like the *Gorgias,* the *Phaedrus* too favors order, harmony, and balance in the human soul; but it seeks to attain this goal chiefly through correctly directing the soul's erotic love (at best a type of divine madness) for the beautiful. People can acquire good order in their souls by being driven by fear, or drawn up by love; a philosophically developed rhetoric must understand and use both motive forces in their proper places. The philosophically minded person who might develop such rhetoric would be moved chiefly by love of the beautiful.

THE POWER OF RHETORIC FOR PLATO

The *Phaedrus* and the *Gorgias* complement each other in a most significant way in regard to the question of rhetoric's power. Let me begin to reflect on this question by asking: In what aspect of political activity would the philosopher have some advantage in practice? To put it most comprehensively, the philosopher's advantage must be that, unblinded by false opinions and spurious hopes, he can see most clearly and analyze most effectively any political situation.[37] However, political understanding of this kind does not yet amount to practical action. When it comes to such action, I suggest, the philosopher's chief advantage can be expected to lie in the area of rhetoric.[38] How great a political advantage, precisely, is that?

The Sophists, as characterized by Aristotle[39] and as exemplified in this respect for Plato by Gorgias, identify or nearly identify politics with rhetoric. As Leo Strauss puts it, "the Sophists believed or tended to believe in the omnipotence of speech." Xenophon, like Plato and Aristotle, rejected such a view of politics and rhetoric.

> Xenophon speaks of his friend Proxenos, who commanded a contingent in Cyrus's expedition against the king of Persia and who was a pupil of the most famous rhetorician, Gorgias. Xenophon says that Proxenos was an honest man and capable to command gentlemen but could not fill his soldiers with fear of him; he was unable to punish those who were not gentlemen or even to rebuke them. But Xenophon, who was a pupil of Socrates, proved to be a most successful commander precisely because he could manage both gentlemen and nongentlemen. Xenophon, the pupil of Socrates, was under no delusion about the sternness and harshness of politics, about that ingredient of politics which transcends speech.[40]

Can so intelligent a man as Gorgias, so aware of his own interests (and as we see in Plato's dialogue, so aware of dangers from cities hostile to his art of rhetoric), really have ignored this simple fact about the limits of speech's power in politics? In some sense, surely not. But perhaps the sophist—or as we might say, the intellectual—has two deep-seated tendencies: first, to overestimate the political advantage conferred by sharpness of mind; and, second, insufficiently to understand the necessary con-

37. Alexandre Kojève in "Tyranny and Wisdom" sketches three distinctive traits of the philosopher that constitute advantages over the "uninitiate": expertise in dialectic, discussion, argument; freedom from prejudices; and greater openness to reality and hence closer approach to the concrete (whereas others confine themselves more to abstractions, without "being aware of their abstract, even unreal character"); in Strauss, On Tyranny, p. 157.
38. Whether the philosopher chooses to put that advantage to use, and if so, how, are of course separate questions.
39. Aristotle, Nicomachean Ethics 10.1181a14–17.
40. Leo Strauss, "Machiavelli," in Studies in Platonic Political Philosophy (Chicago: University of Chicago Press, 1983), p. 228.

ditions for the pursuit of his own preferred activities. The former tendency was given a classic formulation by Hobbes, following Thucydides:

> Men that distrust their own subtilty, are in tumult, and sedition, better disposed for victory, than they that suppose themselves wise, or crafty. For these love to consult, the other (fearing to be circumvented,) to strike first. And in sedition, men being alwayes in the procincts of battell, to hold together, and use all advantages of force, is a better stratagem, than any that can proceed from subtilty of Wit.[41]

The latter tendency, likewise of central importance to Hobbes's thinking, was powerfully represented in Aristophanes' comic criticism of Socrates in the *Clouds*, where we see a Socrates whose all-absorbing interests in nature, in language, and in thought prevent his taking seriously the political and moral concerns of the community on whose continued stable and prosperous existence his own activity depended. Intellectuals today, I need hardly add, generally display no greater immunity to these two tendencies than they have in the past.

Plato, like Xenophon and Aristotle, is acutely aware of rhetoric's limited power in politics and reflects profoundly on the fact. But does he not agree with the sophistic rhetoricians at least so far as to recognize that artful persuasion can have great power? Are not the Sophists correct that, at least in normal circumstances, rhetoric plays a key role in gaining political office and in bringing about one result in a political deliberation (or in a judicial proceeding) rather than another? I believe that Plato would accept this assertion, but he would place greater emphasis than the Sophists do, in his understanding of politics, on what in any given situation limits the range within which rhetorical persuasiveness can have effect.

What the power of rhetoric can achieve at any specified time and place is limited in several ways. Most obviously, the dimension of force (and what may guide the use of force, such as passionate pursuit of one's self-interest) in politics limits what persuasion can accomplish: Polemarchus's suggestion that you cannot persuade those who will not listen remains forever relevant. No less important as limits are a society's existing authoritative opinions and prevailing beliefs. That dimension of political or social

41. Thomas Hobbes, *Leviathan*, ed. C. B. Macpherson (Harmondsworth: Penguin Books, 1968), p. 163; cf. Thucydides 3.83.3–4, which Hobbes paraphrases.

reality's limiting the power of rhetoric is what underlies Socrates' observation in the *Apology* that one way to persuade his audience would be easier than another (even though that other is true). The existing beliefs that
are crucial in these respects involve people's ordering of the human goods
(such as the relative worth of money, health, fame, virtue, knowledge),
their views of what beings are higher than human beings and their affairs
(the divine, god, or gods), and the relationships between these two sets of
beliefs. In only one day, even the most skilled rhetor can hardly succeed in
persuading people contrary to powerfully and deeply held beliefs.

But could not rhetoric have substantially greater power if persuasion is
exerted over a much longer period of time? Could a long-term rhetorical
effort over many generations bring about much greater effects through
profoundly changing people's opinions and beliefs? The example of how
later Greek thinkers understood Homer's influence illustrates the possibility of seriously entertaining such an enterprise. Socrates, for instance,
speaks of "praisers of Homer who say that this poet educated Greece."[42]
Plato, I suggest, intends just such an educational enterprise, under the direction, of course, of Socratic or Platonic philosophy.

The *Gorgias* makes clear the political and moral need for such a project
of reforming prevailing beliefs and limns key features of the substance of
preferable ones. The *Phaedrus* explores how to understand what can make
rhetoric effective and hence how a philosophic art of rhetoric could be developed. The *Phaedrus* culminates in a discussion of writing because writing appears indispensable if an enterprise is to pursue a determined course
over many generations. Thus Plato sketches the possibility of a prolonged
rhetorical project conducted by philosophy for its own benefit as well as
for that of political society. A philosophically inspired and directed rhetoric
of this sort would be a political philosophy, which, for reasons that both
the *Gorgias* and the *Phaedrus* help to clarify, may sometimes resemble myth-
ology or theology. The thoughtful reader of the *Gorgias* will not likely be
surprised to read in Plato's last and longest dialogue that the Athenian
Stranger presents an extensive theology in the context of discussing penal
legislation.[43]

---

42. Plato, *Republic* 10.606e.
43. Plato, *The Laws* 10.

Gorgias

DRAMATIS PERSONAE: CALLICLES, SOCRATES, CHAEREPHON, GORGIAS, POLUS

447a CALLICLES:[1] In war and battle, they say, one must take part in this manner, Socrates.[2]

SOCRATES: Oh, so have we then come, as the saying goes, after the feast, and too late?[3]

CAL.: Yes, and a very urbane feast indeed; for Gorgias just a little while ago made a display for us of many fine things.[4]

---

1. Concerning Callicles, a young man near the beginning of his political career (see 515a), no record survives beyond what appears here. For this reason, many surmise that he may be one of the Platonic dialogues' relatively few fictitious characters. His name suggests beautiful fame or fame for beauty (see comment on *kalos* in note 4). Contradictory indications, unusual for Plato, make it impossible to determine a dramatic date for this dialogue: see most notably 470d and 503c and notes there.

2. The very first word of this dialogue on rhetoric is *war*.

3. Socrates evokes some Greek proverb that reminds the English reader of Falstaff's lines at the end of scene 2, act 4 of *The First Part of King Henry IV:* "To the latter end of a fray and the beginning of a feast / Fits a dull fighter and a keen guest."

4. The extant remains of Gorgias's speeches are mainly display or show pieces, what Aristotle calls epideictic rhetoric (also often called ceremonial). In the subsequent search for a definition of rhetoric, Socrates steers Gorgias away from epideictic toward political (or deliberative) and above all toward forensic rhetoric (to use Aristotle's terms again). Gorgias, a citizen of Leontini, about fourteen years older than Socrates, was one of the most famous teachers of rhetoric. Meno in Plato's dialogue of that name praises Gorgias for eschewing any claim to teach virtue (95c). Socrates names Gorgias as one of three examples of itinerant educators of the young in the *Apology* (19e).

The adjective *kalos* has the basic meaning "beautiful," with a wide range of meanings including "fine" and "noble." I have used all three in different contexts. (In the *Phaedrus* I

soc.: For this, Callicles, Chaerephon[5] here is to blame, since he forced us to fritter our time away in the agora.

447b   CHAEREPHON: No matter, Socrates; for I shall cure it too. For Gorgias is a friend of mine, so that he will make a display for us now, if that seems good, or afterwards, if you wish.

CAL.: What's this, Chaerephon? Does Socrates desire to listen to Gorgias?

CHAE.: We are here for just this very purpose.

CAL.: Well then, whenever you wish to come over to my place—for Gorgias is staying with me and will make a display for you.

soc.: What you say is good, Callicles. But then, would he be willing

447c   to talk with us?[6] For I wish to learn from him what the power of the man's art[7] is, and what it is that he professes and teaches. As for the other thing, the display, let him put it off until afterwards, as you are saying.

CAL.: There's nothing like asking the man himself, Socrates. And indeed this was one aspect of his display; just now at any rate he was calling upon anyone of those inside to ask whatever he might wish, and he said he would answer everything.

soc.: What you say is fine indeed. Chaerephon, ask him!

CHAE.: What shall I ask?

447d   soc.: Who he is.

CHAE.: How do you mean that?

soc.: Just as if he happened to be a craftsman of shoes, he would answer you, I suppose, "a cobbler." Or don't you understand what I'm saying?

CHAE.: I understand and I'll ask. Tell me, Gorgias, is what Callicles

---

have done likewise, but there I use "beautiful" wherever possible.) Another word that means "noble," *gennaios*, I have rendered "nobly born," to distinguish from "noble" meaning *kalos* and to emphasize its etymological connection with birth, generation, descent.

5. Chaerephon is depicted by Aristophanes as Socrates' chief sidekick in the *Clouds*, and Plato has Socrates in the *Apology* relate that the impulsive, democratic Chaerephon inquired of the Delphic oracle whether there was anyone wiser than Socrates.

6. *Dialegesthai*, to converse, discuss, talk with, occurs here for the first time. It is related to *dialogos* (discussion, conversation, dialogue), to *dialektikos* (conversational, dialectical), etc., all which become themes of discussion later on, especially (as here) in comparison with rhetoric.

7. The Greek *technē* covers a broad range of meanings: art, skill, knowledge, craft, any ordered and teachable body of knowledge (productive, practical, or, sometimes, theoretical). The criteria for an art are discussed later, as in several places in Plato's dialogues. The word "man" here is the emphatically male *anēr*, not the more generic *anthrōpos*, which I have translated "human being " when possible.

here says true, that you profess to answer whatever anyone asks you?

448a GORGIAS: True, Chaerephon. I was just now making exactly those professions; and I say that no one has yet asked me anything new for many years.

CHAE.: Then doubtless you answer easily, Gorgias.

GOR.: You may test this by experiment, Chaerephon.

POLUS:[8] By Zeus, Chaerephon, test me, if you wish! For Gorgias seems to me to be tired out indeed, for he has just gone through many things.

CHAE.: What, Polus? Do you think you'll give finer answers than Gorgias?

448b POL.: And what of it, if they are sufficient for you?

CHAE.: Nothing. So since you wish, answer.

POL.: Ask.

CHAE.: I'm asking now. If Gorgias happened to be a knower of his brother Herodicus's art, what would we justly name him? Wouldn't it be what that one is named?

POL.: Certainly.

CHAE.: In asserting that he is a doctor, then, we would be saying something fine.

POL.: Yes.

CHAE.: And if he were experienced in the art of Aristophon the son of Aglaophon or of his brother,[9] what would we rightly call him?

448c POL.: A painter, clearly.

CHAE.: Now then, since he is a knower of what art, what would we call him to call him rightly?

POL.: Chaerephon, many arts have been discovered among men experimentally through experiences. For experience causes our life to proceed by art, whereas inexperience causes it to proceed by chance. Of each of these arts, various men variously partake of various ones, and the best men partake of the best; among these is Gorgias here, and he has a share in the finest of the arts.

448d SOC.: Polus appears to have equipped himself finely for speeches,[10] Gorgias; however, he isn't doing what he promised Chaerephon.

---

8. Younger than Socrates, a student of Gorgias, and like his teacher a foreigner in Athens (see 487a–b), Polus was a teacher of rhetoric and author of a treatise.

9. The more famous painter Polygnotus.

10. *Logos* has a broad range of meaning: speech in general, including talk or conversation; a formal, ordered speech; a reasoned speech as compared for instance to myth (see 523a); a

GOR.: How so, in particular, Socrates?

SOC.: He doesn't really appear to me to be answering what is asked.

GOR.: Well then you ask him, if you wish.

SOC.: No, at least not if you wish to answer yourself; it would be much more pleasant to ask you. For it is clear to me even from what he has said that Polus has practiced what is called rhetoric[11] rather than conversing.

448e POL.: How so, Socrates?

SOC.: Because, Polus, when Chaerephon asks of what art Gorgias is a knower, you extol his art as if someone were blaming it, but you did not answer what it is.

POL.: Didn't I answer that it was the finest?

SOC.: Very much so indeed. But no one asked what sort of art Gorgias's was, but what art, and what one ought to call Gorgias. Just as Chaerephon offered earlier examples and you answered him finely 449a and briefly, so now too say what art it is and what we must call Gorgias. Or rather, Gorgias, you tell us yourself what one must call you, as a knower of what art.

GOR.: Of rhetoric, Socrates.

SOC.: Then one must call you a rhetor?[12]

GOR.: And a good one, Socrates, if you wish to call me what I boast that I am, as Homer said.[13]

SOC.: But I do wish.

GOR.: Then call me so.

449b SOC.: So then should we assert that you are able to make others rhetors too?

GOR.: This indeed is what I proclaim, not only here but elsewhere too.

SOC.: Would you be willing then, Gorgias, to continue just as we are talking now, asking and answering, and to put off until afterwards

---

rational account or argument; reasoning itself. The connection between speech and reason suggested by the word *logos* plays an important role at several points in the arguments.

11. Socrates makes the first explicit mention of the dialogue's theme. The noun *rhētōr* means speaker, orator, rhetor (sometimes with the implication good speaker); the adjective *rhētorikos* means skilled in speaking, rhetorical, or (designating a person) rhetorician; with the feminine singular *rhētorikē* one supplies *technē* (or perhaps in certain contexts *epistēmē*) to understand the rhetorical art (or science), rhetoric.

12. *Rhētōr* can designate someone knowledgeable about speaking (whom one would tend to call a rhetorician) or a politician or statesman whose leadership stems from his speaking (whom one might want to call an orator); I avoid deciding each case by using the term "rhetor."

13. This stock Homeric formula can be found at *Iliad* 6.211, for instance.

this lengthiness of speech that Polus started? Don't play false with what you promise, but be willing to answer what is asked briefly.

GOR.: Some answers, Socrates, must necessarily be made in speeches of great length; but I shall nevertheless try, at least, to speak as briefly

449c   as possible. For indeed this too is one of the things I assert, that no one could say the same things in briefer speeches than I.

SOC.: That is just what's needed, Gorgias. Make a display for me of precisely this, brief speaking, and put off the lengthy speaking until afterwards.

GOR.: I shall do so, and you will assert you've heard no one briefer of speech.

SOC.: Well then. You assert that you are a knower of the art of rheto-

449d   ric and could make another a rhetor as well. What, of the things that are, does rhetoric happen to be about? Just as weaving is about the production of clothing; isn't it?

GOR.: Yes.

SOC.: And then music is about the making of tunes?

GOR.: Yes.

SOC.: By Hera,[14] Gorgias, I admire the answers, how you answer through the briefest ones possible!

GOR.: Indeed I think, Socrates, that I'm doing this quite suitably.

SOC.: What you say is good. Come then, answer me in this manner about rhetoric as well: about what, of the things that are, is it a science?

449e   GOR.: About speeches.

SOC.: What sort of speeches, Gorgias? Those that make clear to the sick by what way of life they would be healthy?

GOR.: No.

SOC.: Then rhetoric is not about *all* speeches.

GOR.: No, it's not.

SOC.: Yet it does make men able to speak.

GOR.: Yes.

SOC.: And therefore able also to understand what they are speaking about?

GOR.: Indeed, how could it not?

450a   SOC.: Well then, does the medical art that we were just now talking about make men able to understand and speak about the sick?

14. Hera, wife of Zeus, seems to be named as an oath most often by women.

GOR.: Necessarily.

SOC.: Then medicine too, as it seems, is about speeches.

GOR.: Yes.

SOC.: Those about diseases?

GOR.: Very much so.

SOC.: So then, is gymnastic too about speeches, those about the good and bad condition of bodies?

GOR.: Certainly.

SOC.: And indeed such is the case with the other arts too, Gorgias.
450b Each of them is about those speeches that happen to be about the business of which each is the art.

GOR.: Apparently.

SOC.: Why in the world then don't you call the other arts rhetorical, seeing that they are about speeches, if indeed you call this one rhetoric because it is about speeches?

GOR.: Because, Socrates, the whole science, one might say, of the other arts is concerned with manual skill and such actions, whereas in rhetoric there is no such handiwork, but its whole action and decisive ef-
450c fect are through speeches. For these reasons I claim that the art of rhetoric is concerned with speeches, and what I say is right, as I assert.

SOC.: So am I then beginning to understand what sort of thing you wish to call it? Well, perhaps I shall know more clearly. Answer then: we have arts, don't we?

GOR.: Yes.

SOC.: Now, taking all the arts, in some of them, I think, working is the major part and they need little[15] speech (and some need no speech), but the business of the art would be accomplished even in silence,
450d such as painting and sculpting and many others. You seem to me to mean such arts, with which you say rhetoric has nothing to do. Isn't that so?

GOR.: Your apprehension, Socrates, is certainly fine indeed.

SOC.: And then there are other arts that accomplish everything through speech, and need in addition almost no work or very little, such as arithmetic, calculation, and geometry, yes, and draught playing[16] and many other arts. In some of these the speeches are approximately equal to the actions, but in many the speeches are greater,

15. "Little" here (and in Socrates' next speech) translates the same word that he used earlier in calling for "brief speaking."
16. A game that appears to have resembled checkers, played with partners against opponents (see *Republic* 333d). It seems often in Plato to be an image of dialectic, with the setting

450e   and absolutely their whole action and decisive effect[17] are through
       speeches. You seem to me to be saying that rhetoric is one of the arts
       of this sort.

       GOR.: What you say is true.

       SOC.: But I do not think you wish to call any one of these rhetoric,
       notwithstanding that in your verbal statement you said that the art
       that has its decisive effect through speech is rhetoric, and someone
       might retort, if he wished to make difficulties in the argument, "Do
       you then say, Gorgias, that arithmetic is rhetoric?" But I do not think
       you are saying that either arithmetic or geometry is rhetoric.

451a   GOR.: What you think is right, Socrates, and your apprehension is just.

       SOC.: Come now, you too; provide a complete answer in the way I
       asked.[18] Since rhetoric happens to be one of those arts that use speech
       for the most part, and other arts too happen to be of the same sort, try
       to say what rhetoric, which has its decisive effect in speeches, is
       about. Just as if someone asked me about any one of the arts that we

451b   were just now talking about, "Socrates, what is the art of arithmetic?"
       I should say to him, just as you recently did, that it is one of those that
       have their decisive effect through speech. And if he asked me further,
       "What are they about?" I should say it is one of those that are about
       the even and the odd, however large each happens to be. And again,
       if he asked, "What art do you call calculation?" I should say that it
       too is one of those that accomplish their whole decisive effect by
       speech. And if he asked further, "What is it about?" I should say, just

451c   like those who write up proposals in the people's assembly,[19] that in
       other respects calculation is just like arithmetic (for it is about the
       same thing, the even and the odd), but it differs to this extent, that
       calculation examines how great the odd and the even are in relation

---

down and movement of pieces resembling the positing and changing of suppositions in
discussion.

17. "Decisive effect" translates *to kuros,* whose more basic meaning is supreme power or
authority. The same translation was used at 450b for the less common *hē kurōsis,* which can
mean ratification.

18. The translation follows Dodds's correction (E. R. Dodds, *Plato; Gorgias* [A Revised Text
with Introduction and Commentary] [Oxford: Clarendon Press, 1959]; the chief manuscript
reading would appear to mean "provide a complete answer to what I asked."

19. Later on Socrates starkly opposes his concerns and ways to those characteristic of politics, but here he compares his procedure to the work of politicians drafting proposed legislation. Perhaps he thus gently steers the conversation about rhetoric away from display
speeches and toward political rhetoric. Writing or composing legislation plays a brief but
crucial role in Socrates' discussion of writing in the *Phaedrus,* at 257c–258d, 277d, and
278c–e.

to themselves and to one another. And if someone asked about astronomy, and if, when I said that it too accomplishes all its decisive effects by speech, he said "What, Socrates, are the speeches of astronomy about?" I should say that they are about what speed the motions of stars, sun, and moon have in relation to one another.

GOR.: What you would say is right, Socrates.

451d SOC.: Come then, you too, Gorgias. For rhetoric happens to be one of the arts that carry out and accomplish all their decisive effects by speech, isn't it?

GOR.: That is so.

SOC.: Then say, what are those arts about? Of the things that are, what is this thing that these speeches used by rhetoric are about?

GOR.: The greatest of human affairs, Socrates, and the best.

SOC.: But what you are saying now, Gorgias, is also debatable and
451e is as yet nothing distinct. For I think that in drinking parties you have heard human beings singing this song, in which they enumerate in song that "being healthy is best, and second is to have become beautiful, and third," as the poet who wrote the song says, "is being wealthy without fraud."[20]

GOR.: I have heard it; but to what purpose do you say this?

452a SOC.: Because if at this moment the craftsmen of those things praised by him who made the song stood by you—the doctor, the trainer, and the moneymaker—and first the doctor said, "Socrates, Gorgias is deceiving you; for his art is not concerned with the greatest good for human beings, but mine is." If then I asked him, "Who are you that say these things?" he would probably say that he was a doctor. "What then are you saying? Is the work of your art the greatest good?" "How could it not be, Socrates," he would probably say, "since its
452b work is health? What is a greater good for human beings than health?" And if after him the trainer in turn said, "I too should be amazed, Socrates, if Gorgias can display for you a greater good of his art than I can of mine," I should in turn say to him as well, "You then, who are you, human being, and what is your work?" "A trainer," he would say, "and my work is making human beings beautiful and strong in body." After the trainer, the moneymaker would speak, de-

---

20. On the qualification "without fraud," compare philosophizing without fraud at *Phaedrus* 249a. Dodds gives the full quatrain as quoted by the scholiast and notes that Socrates omits the song's fourth good, "to be in the prime of youth with friends." Socrates also drops the specification *phuan* from the third good: "beautiful in one's nature (growth, stature)."

spising everyone very much, as I think: "Only look, Socrates, if any-
452c thing manifests itself to you as a greater good than wealth, whether
in Gorgias's possession or anybody else's." We should then say to
him, "What's that? Are you a craftsman of this?" He would say yes.
"Who are you?" "A moneymaker." "What then? Do you judge wealth
to be the greatest good for human beings?" we will say. "How could
it not be?" he will say. "And yet Gorgias here disputes that, arguing
that the art in his possession is the cause of greater good than yours,"
we should say. So it is clear that after this he would ask, "And what
452d is this good? Let Gorgias answer!" Come then, Gorgias: considering
yourself asked both by those men and by me, answer what this is
which you say is the greatest good for human beings and of which
you are a craftsman.

GOR.: That which is in truth, Socrates, the greatest good and the cause
both of freedom for human beings themselves and at the same time
of rule over others in each man's own city.[21]

SOC.: What then do you say this is?

452e GOR.: I for one say it is being able to persuade by speeches judges in
the law court, councillors in the council, assemblymen in the assembly, and in every other gathering whatsoever, when there is a political gathering.[22] And indeed with this power you will have the doctor
as your slave, and the trainer as your slave; and that moneymaker
of yours will be plainly revealed to be making money for another
and not for himself, but for you who can speak and persuade multitudes.

SOC.: You seem to me now, Gorgias, very nearly to have made clear
453a what art you consider rhetoric to be, and if I understand anything,
you're saying that rhetoric is a craftsman of persuasion, and its whole
occupation and chief point ends in this. Or do you have anything further to say, which rhetoric can produce in the soul of the listeners, in
addition to persuasion?

---

21. In Thucydides 3.45.6, Diodotus calls the greatest things freedom and rule over others.
"City" translates *polis*, the self-sufficient, independent political community.
22. The notion of a law court as a political gathering would make obvious sense to an ancient Greek accustomed to large juries (or assemblies of judges), like the five hundred who
heard the accusation against Socrates and found him guilty. In Socrates' suggested definition of rhetoric at *Phaedrus* 561a–b, rhetoric is emphatically not limited to addressing political groups. One imagines that Gorgias himself has intellectual interests beyond the political, but doubtless he singles out rhetoric's political power here to appeal to the chief
concern of potential students.

GOR.: Not at all, Socrates; you seem to me to define it adequately, for this is its chief point.

SOC.: Now listen, Gorgias. For I—know it well—as I persuade myself,
453b if ever anyone talks with someone else wishing to know the very thing that the speech is about, I too am one of these people, and I deem that you are too.

GOR.: What then, Socrates?

SOC.: Now I'll tell you. Know well that I do not distinctly know what in the world this persuasion from rhetoric is of which you are speaking, and what matters the persuasion is about—not but that I have a suspicion, at least, of what I think you are saying it is and what things it is about. But I shall nonetheless ask you what in the world you say
453c this persuasion from rhetoric is, and what things it is about. On account of what do I, who have a suspicion, ask you and not say myself? Not on account of you, but on account of the argument, in order that it may go forward so as to make what is being talked about as manifest as possible to us. Now consider if I seem to you to question you justly: just as if I happened to be asking you who Zeuxis is among painters, if you said to me that he was one who painted living beings, wouldn't I justly ask you, one who painted what kinds of living beings and where?

GOR.: Certainly.

453d SOC.: Would it be for this reason, that there are other painters too, who paint many other living beings?

GOR.: Yes.

SOC.: But if no one other than Zeuxis painted,[23] your answer would have been fine?

GOR.: How could it not be?

SOC.: Come then, speak about rhetoric as well. Does rhetoric alone seem to you to produce persuasion or do other arts too? I am saying something of this sort: whenever anyone teaches any subject at all, does the one who teaches persuade or not?

GOR.: Absolutely yes, Socrates; he persuades most of all.

453e SOC.: Then let us speak again on the same arts as just now. Doesn't arithmetic teach us as many things as belong to number, and the arithmetical man does too?

---

23. The verb for "painted" here is *graphein,* to write; the word translated "painter" has the roots "write" and "living" (or life, alive, animal). On possible links among rhetoric, writing, and painting, see *Phaedrus* 275d.

GOR.: Certainly.

SOC.: And so it persuades too?

GOR.: Yes.

SOC.: Then arithmetic too is a craftsman of persuasion?

GOR.: Apparently.

SOC.: So then if someone asks us what sort of persuasion, and about what, we shall probably answer him that it is didactic, about the even 454a and the odd, however large. And for all the other arts that we were just now talking about, we shall be able to show that they are craftsmen of persuasion, and what the persuasion is, and about what, won't we?

GOR.: Yes.

SOC.: Therefore rhetoric is not the only craftsman of persuasion.

GOR.: What you say is true.

SOC.: Since, therefore, not it alone but also others achieve this work, just as concerning the painter, we might after this justly ask the speaker further, "Of what sort of persuasion, and of persuasion about what, is rhetoric the art?" Or doesn't it seem to you just to ask further? 454b GOR.: It does to me, at any rate.

SOC.: Answer then, Gorgias, since it seems so to you too.

GOR.: I say then, Socrates, persuasion in law courts and in other mobs, as I was saying just a moment ago, and about those things that are just and unjust.[24]

SOC.: And surely I had a suspicion that you meant this persuasion, and about these things, Gorgias. But so that you may not be amazed if again a little later I ask you some other such thing, which seems to 454c be clear but which I ask about further—for, as I said, I ask for the sake of the argument's being brought to a conclusion in a consequential manner, not on account of you but so that we may not become accustomed to guessing and hastily snatching up each other's words, but so that you may bring your own views to a conclusion in accord with what you set down, in whatever way you wish.

GOR.: And in my opinion, Socrates, you are doing so rightly, at any rate.

SOC.: Come then, let us examine this as well. Do you call one thing "to have learned?"

24. Gorgias, perhaps still constrained by Socrates' demand for brevity, further narrows the focus of rhetoric here—perhaps also to emphasize a forensic rhetoric that is most in demand from students (consider Aristophanes' *Clouds*, vv. 98–99 and passim).

GOR.: Yes I do.

SOC.: And how about "to have believed?"

454d GOR.: I do.

SOC.: Now, do having learned and having believed, and learning and belief,[25] seem to you to be the same thing, or something different?

GOR.: Different, Socrates, I certainly think.

SOC.: Indeed, what you think is fine; and you will perceive it from this. For if someone asked you, "Is there, Gorgias, a false belief and a true one?" you would, as I think, say yes.

GOR.: Yes.

SOC.: And what about this: Is there false and true knowledge?

GOR.: Not at all.

SOC.: It is clear, therefore, that they are not the same thing.

GOR.: What you say is true.

454e SOC.: But surely both those who have learned and those who have believed are persuaded.

GOR.: That is so.

SOC.: Do you wish us then to set down two forms[26] of persuasion, one that provides belief without knowing, and one that provides knowledge?

GOR.: Certainly.

SOC.: Which persuasion, then, does rhetoric produce in law courts and the other mobs, about just and unjust things? The one from which believing comes into being without knowing, or the one from which knowing comes?

GOR.: It's clear, I suppose, Socrates, that it's the one from which believing comes.

455a SOC.: Rhetoric, then, as seems likely, is a craftsman of belief-inspiring but not didactic persuasion about the just and the unjust.[27]

GOR.: Yes.

25. *Pistis*, belief (or conviction, trust) is used in the *Republic* to name the second part of the divided line (the level of our sense perceptions). Here it is distinguished from *mathēsis*.

26. The word is *eidos*, which means the looks, the form, the class character of a thing. I have translated it "form" wherever possible, and noted any variation from that. I have simply transliterated the related word *idea*. *Eidos* and *idea* designate the objects of genuine knowledge in, for example, *Republic* 7.

27. "Didactic" and "to teach" stem from the same root in Greek.

Struck by Socrates' open attack on rhetors a bit further on, one easily overlooks his own important resemblance to them. Given his often-admitted lack of knowledge and his denial that he teaches (e.g., at *Apology* 33a), he could be understood, like them, to produce nondidactic persuasion.

soc.: The rhetor, therefore, is not didactic with law courts and the other mobs about just and unjust things, but persuasive only; for he would not be able, I suppose, to teach so large a mob such great matters in a short time.[28]

gor.: Indeed not.

soc.: Come then, let us see what we are really saying about rhetoric;
455b for indeed I am myself as yet unable fully to understand what I am saying. When the city has a gathering concerned with the choice of doctors or shipwrights or some other craftsmanlike tribe, the rhetorician then will not give counsel, will he? For it is clear that in each choice one must choose the most artful. Nor when it concerns the building of walls or the preparation of harbors and dockyards, but rather architects; nor, again, when there is deliberation about the
455c choice of generals or some disposition of troops against enemies or the seizing of territories, but then those skilled in generalship will give counsel, and rhetoricians will not. Or what do you say, Gorgias, about such things? For since you say that you are yourself a rhetor and make others rhetoricians, it is well to learn the things of your art from you. And consider that I am now eagerly promoting your affair too. For perhaps some one of those inside happens to wish to become a student of yours, as I perceive some, indeed quite a large num-
455d ber, who perhaps would be ashamed to ask you. So, being asked by me, consider that you are asked by them too: "What will be ours, Gorgias, if we associate with you? About what things will we be able to give counsel to the city? About the just and unjust alone, or also about the things of which Socrates was speaking just now?" So try to answer them.

gor.: I shall indeed try, Socrates, clearly to uncover for you the whole power of rhetoric; for you yourself have beautifully led the way. For
455e you know, I suppose, that these dockyards and the Athenians' walls and the preparation of the harbors came into being from Themistocles' counsel, and others from Pericles',[29] but not from the craftsmen.

28. Could one imagine a more tactful way of bringing up the rhetor's lack of concern for conveying knowledge about issues of justice? At *Apology* 37a–b, Socrates explains his own failure to persuade his judges through the shortness of time available and praises the practice elsewhere of allowing several days for a capital case. On the importance of adequate time for judicial proceedings, see *Laws* 766e.
29. Gorgias gives as examples the leading founder and the most prominent developer of Athens's imperial power. See Thucydides' accounts and judgments of these figures in books 1 and 2 of his *History of the Peloponnesian War*.

soc.: These things are said, Gorgias, about Themistocles; and Pericles I heard myself when he gave us counsel about the middle wall.

456a gor.: And whenever there is a choice involving the things you were just now speaking of, Socrates, you see that the rhetors are the ones who give counsel and victoriously carry their resolutions about these things.

soc.: And it is in amazement at these things, Gorgias, that I have long been asking what in the world the power of rhetoric is. For it manifestly appears to me as a power demonic in greatness, when I consider it in this way.

gor.: If only you knew the whole of it, Socrates—that it gathers together and holds under itself all powers, so to speak. I shall relate to
456b you a great piece of evidence. On many occasions now I have gone in with my brother and with other doctors to one of the sick who was unwilling either to drink a drug or to submit himself to the doctor for surgery or cautery; the doctor being unable to persuade him, I persuaded him, by no other art than rhetoric. And I assert further that, if a rhetorical man and a doctor should go into any city you wish and should have to contest in speech, in the assembly or in some other
456c gathering, which of the two ought to be chosen doctor, the doctor would plainly be nowhere, but the man with power to speak would be chosen, if he wished. And if he should contest against any other craftsman whatsoever, the rhetorician rather than anyone else would persuade them to choose himself. For there is nothing about which the rhetorician would not speak more persuasively than any other of the craftsmen in a multitude. The power of the art, then, is so great and of such a sort; one must, however, use rhetoric, Socrates, just as every
456d other competitive skill. For one must not use other competitive skills against all human beings on this account, that one has learned boxing and *pankration*[30] and fighting in heavy armor, so as to be stronger than both friends and enemies—one must not on this account either beat or stab and kill friends. Nor, by Zeus, if someone who has frequented a wrestling-school, is in good bodily condition, and has become skilled in boxing, then beats his father and mother or some
456e other relative or friend, one must not on this account hate the trainers and those who teach fighting in heavy armor, and expel them

---

30. *Pankration,* whose roots mean "all" and "power," was a combination of wrestling and boxing.

from the cities. For they imparted their skill to these men to use justly against enemies and doers of injustice, in defending themselves, not

457a in starting something: but these men, perverting it, use the might and the art incorrectly. Those who taught are therefore not base, nor is the art either blameworthy or base on this account, but, I think, those who do not use it correctly. The very same argument applies to rhetoric as well. For the rhetor has power to speak against all men and

457b about everything, so as to be more persuasive in multitudes about, in brief, whatever he wishes; but it nonetheless does not follow that one must on this account deprive the doctors of reputation—for he could do this—nor the other craftsmen, but one must use rhetoric justly too, just as competitive skill. And, I think, if someone has become a rhetorician and then does injustice with this power and art,[31] one must not hate the man who taught him and expel him from the cities. For

457c that man imparted it for just use, and the other used it in the opposite way. It is just, then, to hate, expel, and kill the one who uses it not correctly, but not the one who taught it.

soc.: I think, Gorgias, that you too have had experience of many arguments and have observed in them something of the following sort, that they cannot easily define for each other the things that they en-

457d deavor to talk about, and learn and teach each other, and in this manner break off the conversations; but when they disagree about something and one says the other is not speaking correctly or not clearly, they become sorely angry and think the other is speaking from envy of themselves, loving victory but not seeking the subject proposed in the argument. And some in the end give over most shamefully,[32] having reviled each other and said and heard about themselves such things that even those present are annoyed with themselves, because

457e they thought it worthwhile to become the audience of such human beings. On account of what, then, do I say these things? Because now you seem to me to be saying things not quite consequent upon nor consistent with what you were saying at first about rhetoric. So I'm afraid to refute you, lest you suppose that I speak from love of victory, not in regard to the subject's becoming manifest, but in regard

31. Gorgias's awareness that rhetoric like any other skill may be used unjustly as well as justly is doubtless linked with his reportedly not promising that he taught virtue, unlike other sophists, but even ridiculing that claim (*Meno* 96c).

32. This adverb in the superlative derives from *aischros,* the opposite of *kalos* (see note 4 at 447a); I translate with either "ugly" or "shameful."

458a to you. Now then, if you too are one of the human beings of whom I am also one, I would with pleasure question you further; and if not, I would let it drop. And of what men am I one? Those who are refuted with pleasure if I say something not true, and who refute with pleasure if someone should say something not true—and indeed not with less pleasure to be refuted than to refute. For I consider it a greater good, to the extent that it is a greater good to be released oneself from the greatest evil than to release another. For I think that

458b nothing is so great an evil for a human being as false opinion about the things that our argument now happens to be about. So if you too say you are such a one, let us converse; but if indeed it seems that we must let it drop, let us forthwith bid it farewell and break off the argument.

GOR.: But I say that I myself, Socrates, am also such a one as you indicate; but perhaps we must nevertheless give thought also to the situation of those present. Quite a while ago, you see, before you came, I made a display for those present of many things, and now perhaps we

458c shall prolong it too far, if we converse. We must, then, consider their situation, lest we detain some of them who wish to do something else.

CHAE.: You yourselves, Gorgias and Socrates, hear the uproar[33] from these men, wishing to hear what you'll say. And as for me, may I not have so great a lack of leisure as to pass up such arguments, spoken in such a manner, so that doing something else becomes more important to me!

458d CAL.: By the gods, Chaerephon, yes indeed, and I too have by now been present at many arguments, and I don't know if I have ever had such pleasure as now. So for me, even if you should want to converse the whole day long, you'll be gratifying me.

SOC.: Indeed, Callicles, for my part nothing prevents it, if Gorgias is willing.

GOR.: It would indeed be shameful after all this, Socrates, for me to be unwilling, since I myself made the proclamation to ask whatever any-

458e one wishes. Well then, if it seems good to these men, converse and ask what you wish.

SOC.: Hear then, Gorgias, the things I was amazed at in what you said; for perhaps what you are saying is correct but I am not appre-

---

33. *Thorubos* can be the noise of approval, as here, or of disapproval, like the noise made against certain things that Socrates said at his trial (*Apology* 17d, 20e, 21a, 27b, and 30c).

hending it correctly. Do you say that you can make someone a rhetorician, if he wishes to learn from you?

GOR.: Yes.

SOC.: And so as to be persuasive in a mob about all things, not by teaching but by persuading?

459a GOR.: Yes, certainly.

SOC.: Then you were saying just now that the rhetor will be more persuasive than the doctor even about the healthy.

GOR.: Yes I was—that is, in a mob.

SOC.: So then, does the "in a mob" amount to this: among those who don't know? For among those who know, at any rate, I don't suppose he will be more persuasive than the doctor.

GOR.: What you say is true.

SOC.: So then if he'll be more persuasive than the doctor, does he become more persuasive than the one who knows?

GOR.: Certainly.

459b SOC.: Since he's not a doctor, at any rate; is he?

GOR.: No.

SOC.: And the nondoctor, I suppose, is a nonknower of the things of which the doctor is a knower.

GOR.: Clearly so.

SOC.: The one who does not know, therefore, will be more persuasive than the one who knows among those who don't know, whenever the rhetor is more persuasive than the doctor. Is this what happens, or something else?

GOR.: In this case, at least, that is what happens.

SOC.: So then is the rhetor, and rhetoric, in the same situation in regard to all the other arts as well? It does not at all need to know how
459c the matters themselves stand, but to have discovered a certain device of persuasion so as to appear to know more than those who know, to those who don't know.

GOR.: Does not much ease in doing things thus come about, Socrates, in that one who has not learned the other arts but only this one, in no way gets the worst of it from the craftsmen?

SOC.: Whether the rhetor gets the worst of it or not from the others through being thus, we shall examine presently, if it should have something to do with our argument. But now let us first consider the
459d following. Does the rhetorician happen to be in this same situation in regard to the just and the unjust, the shameful and the noble, and

good and bad, as he is in regard to the healthy and the other things belonging to the other arts: not knowing the things themselves—what is good or what bad or what noble or what shameful or just or unjust—but having devised persuasion about them so as, though not

459e knowing, to seem to know more than the one who knows, among those who don't know? Or is it necessary to know, and must the one who is going to learn rhetoric know these things before coming to you? And if not, will you, the teacher of rhetoric, teach him who comes nothing of these things—for it is not your work—and will you make him who doesn't know such things seem among the many to know, and seem to be good although he isn't? Or will you be wholly unable to teach him rhetoric, unless he knows the truth about these things

460a beforehand? Or what is the case with such things, Gorgias? And by Zeus, uncover rhetoric, as you were recently saying, and say what in the world its power is.

GOR.: Well I think, Socrates, if he happens not to know, he will learn these things too from me.

SOC.: Stop there, for what you say is fine. If you make someone a rhetorician, he must of necessity know the just and the unjust things, either beforehand or by learning them later from you.

GOR.: Certainly.

460b SOC.: What about this, then? Is the one who has learned the things of carpentry a carpenter?

GOR.: Yes.

SOC.: So too, then, is the one who has learned the musical things musical?

GOR.: Yes.

SOC.: And is the one who has learned the medical things a doctor? And thus for the other things according to the same argument, is the one who has learned each set of things such as the science makes each man?

GOR.: Certainly.

SOC.: So then according to this argument, is also the one who has learned the just things just?

GOR.: Quite so, I suppose.

SOC.: And the just man does just things, I suppose.

GOR.: Yes.

460c SOC.: So then is it necessary that the rhetorician be just, and that the just man wish to do just things?

GOR.: Apparently, at least.

SOC.: Therefore the just man will never wish to do injustice.

GOR.: Necessarily.

SOC.: And it's necessary from the argument that the rhetorician be just.

GOR.: Yes.

SOC.: Therefore the rhetorician will never wish to do injustice.

GOR.: Apparently not, at least.[34]

SOC.: Now then, do you remember saying a little while ago that one must not bring charges against the trainers and expel them from the
460d cities, if the boxer uses the art of boxing and does injustice, and thus also, in the same way, if the rhetor uses rhetoric unjustly, one must not bring charges against the one who taught and drive him out of the city, but against the one who does injustice and does not use rhetoric rightly? Were these things said, or not?

GOR.: They were said.

SOC.: But now, at any rate, this same man, the rhetorician, is mani-
460e festly one who would never do injustice. Isn't he?

GOR.: Apparently.

SOC.: And in the first speeches, at least, Gorgias, it was said that rhetoric was concerned with speeches not about the even and odd, but about the just and unjust. Wasn't it?

GOR.: Yes.

SOC.: Accordingly, when you were then saying these things, I supposed that rhetoric would never be an unjust business, since indeed it always makes speeches about justice; but since a little later you
461a said that the rhetor might use rhetoric unjustly as well, I was thus amazed and thought that the things said did not harmonize, and so I made those speeches, that if you thought, just as I do, that it is a gain to be refuted, it would be worthwhile to discuss, but if not, let's bid it farewell. And from our later investigation you too see now for yourself that once again it is agreed that the rhetorician is powerless to use rhetoric unjustly and to want to do injustice. So then, what
461b in the world is the case with these things, by the dog,[35] Gorgias, is a matter for no little conversation, so as to examine it adequately.

POL.: What's this, Socrates? Do you too actually hold such an opinion

---

34. Many editors suspect some interpolation in this apparently over-elaborated set of exchanges, and drop one or two of them.

35. When he uses this unusual oath again at 482b, Socrates indicates that "the dog" was an Egyptian god (the dog-headed god Anubis).

about rhetoric as you are now saying? Or do you think—because Gorgias was ashamed not to agree further with you that the rhetorical man also knows the just, noble, and good things, and if he came to him not knowing these things, that he himself would teach them, and then from this agreement perhaps some contradiction came about

461c in the speeches (this you are really fond of, when you yourself have led people on to such questions)—for who do you think would utterly deny both that he knows the just things and that he would teach others? But it is much rudeness to lead arguments into such things.

soc.: Most noble Polus, surely it is on purpose that we acquire companions and sons, so that when we ourselves, having become older, are tripped up, you younger ones who are present might set our life

461d upright again, both in deeds and in speeches. And so now if Gorgias and I are being tripped up in the speeches on some point, you who are present set us upright—and so you are just—and if something of what has been agreed on seems to you not to have been agreed on finely, I am willing for you to take back whatever you wish,[36] if you guard against only one thing for me.

pol.: What do you mean by this?

soc.: That you confine the lengthiness of speech, Polus, that you attempted to use at first.

pol.: What's this? Will it not be allowed me to say as much as I wish?

461e soc.: You would certainly suffer terrible things, best of men, if you came to Athens, where there is the most freedom to speak in Greece, and then you alone had the misfortune not to get any there. But then set against it this: if you are speaking at length and are unwilling to answer what is asked, would I on the other hand not suffer terrible

462a things, if it will not be allowed me to go away and not to listen to you? But if something in the argument that has been stated bothers you and you wish to set it upright, as I was just now saying, take back what seems good to you, and, in your turn asking and being asked, just as Gorgias and I, refute and be refuted. For you assert, I suppose, that you too know the things that Gorgias knows, don't you?

pol.: I do.

soc.: So then do you too on each occasion bid one to ask you whatever one wishes, on the grounds that you know what to answer?

pol.: Yes, certainly.

462b soc.: And now then, do whichever of these you wish, ask or answer.

36. The phrase appears to be a metaphor from draught playing; see note at 450d.

POL.: Well, I shall do this. And answer me, Socrates: since Gorgias in your opinion is at a loss concerning rhetoric, what do you say it is?

SOC.: Are you then asking me what art I say it is?

POL.: I am.

SOC.: In my opinion at least, it is no art, Polus, to tell you the truth.

POL.: But what in your opinion is rhetoric?

SOC.: A business that you say makes art,[37] in the writing that I have

462c lately read.

POL.: What do you mean by this?

SOC.: I mean a certain experience.

POL.: Then rhetoric in your opinion is experience?

SOC.: In my opinion, at any rate, unless you say something else.

POL.: Experience of what?

SOC.: Of the production of a certain grace and pleasure.

POL.: So then isn't rhetoric in your opinion a fine thing, since it's able to gratify human beings?

SOC.: What, Polus? Have you already learned from me what I say it

462d is, so that you are asking what comes after this, if it isn't fine in my opinion?

POL.: Well, haven't I learned that you say it is a certain experience?

SOC.: Do you wish then, since you honor gratifying, to gratify me in a small matter?

POL.: I do.

SOC.: Ask me now, what art is cookery in my opinion.

POL.: I am asking then, what art is cookery?

SOC.: No art, Polus. Well, say, "But what is it?"

POL.: I am saying it.

SOC.: A certain experience. Say, "Of what?"

POL.: I am saying it.

462e SOC.: Of the production of grace and pleasure, Polus.

POL.: Is cookery therefore the same thing as rhetoric?

SOC.: Not at all, but certainly a part of the same pursuit.

POL.: What pursuit do you say this is?

SOC.: I'm afraid it may be rather rude to tell the truth; indeed I shrink from speaking on account of Gorgias, lest he think I am satirizing[38] his pursuit. But whether the rhetoric that Gorgias pursues is this, I

---

37. Dodds argues for an alternative meaning: a business "of which you claim to have made an art in your treatise."

38. The Greek word (*diakōmōdein*) contains the word for "comedy."

463a do not know—for from our recent argument, what in the world he considers it to be did not at all become manifest to us—but what I call rhetoric is part of a certain business that is not one of the fine ones.

GOR.: What business, Socrates? Speak, without feeling ashamed before me.

SOC.: In my opinion, then, Gorgias, it is a certain pursuit that is not artful but belongs to a soul that is skilled at guessing, courageous,[39] and terribly clever by nature at associating with human beings; and

463b I call its chief point flattery. Of this pursuit there are, in my opinion, many various parts, and one of them is cookery; it seems to be an art, but—as my argument goes—is not an art but experience and routine. I also call rhetoric a part of this pursuit, and cosmetic too and sophistry, these four parts directed to four kinds of business. So then if

463c Polus wishes to learn, let him learn; for he has not yet learned what sort of part of flattery I say rhetoric is, but my not yet answering has escaped his notice, and he is asking further whether I do not consider it to be a fine thing. But I shall not answer him whether I consider rhetoric to be a fine or a shameful thing before I first answer what it is. For it's not just, Polus; but if you wish to learn, ask what sort of part of flattery I say rhetoric is.

POL.: I am asking then, so answer what sort of part.

463d SOC.: Well now, would you then understand when I've answered? For rhetoric according to my argument is a phantom of a part of politics.[40]

POL.: What then? Do you say it is a fine or a shameful thing?

SOC.: I say shameful—for I call bad things shameful—since I must answer you as if you already knew what I'm saying.

GOR.: But by Zeus, Socrates, even I myself do not comprehend what you're saying!

463e SOC.: Quite likely, Gorgias, for I am not yet saying anything clear, but Polus here is young and swift.[41]

---

39. *Andreios*, "courageous," comes from *anēr*, an emphatically male man, and might well be translated "manly." *Anthrōpos* (which at the cost of occasional awkwardness I have translated "human being") refers more broadly to any member of the human species.

40. *Politikē* could also be translated "statesmanship" or "the political art." Because Socrates is calling into question whether a given pursuit is or is not an art, I have at this point preferred "politics" so as to leave the question open for now.

41. Socrates' reference to youth and swiftness may evoke a pun on Polus's name, which means "colt."

GOR.: Well, leave him be, and tell me what you mean in saying that rhetoric is a phantom of a part of politics.

SOC.: Well, I shall try to declare what rhetoric is, as it appears to me; and if it happens not to be this, Polus here will refute it. You call

464a something body, I suppose, and soul?

GOR.: Indeed, how could I not?

SOC.: So then, do you also think there is a certain good condition of each of these?

GOR.: I do.

SOC.: What about this? Do you think there is a good condition that seems to be, but is not? I mean, for instance, something of this sort: many seem to be in good bodily condition, whom one would not easily perceive not to be in good condition, but a doctor and one of those skilled in gymnastic would.

GOR.: What you say is true.

SOC.: I say that such a thing exists both in body and in soul, which makes the body and the soul seem to be in good condition, but they

464b nonetheless are not.

GOR.: These things are so.

SOC.: Now then, if I can, I shall more clearly display to you what I'm saying. Since there are two kinds of business, I say there are two arts. The one directed to the soul I call politics; the one directed to the body I am unable to name for you in this way, but I say that, while the care of the body is one, it has two parts, gymnastic and medicine; and that of politics, the legislative art is comparable to gymnastic,

464c and justice[42] is the counterpart to medicine. On the one hand, each of these two share something in common with each other, seeing that they are about the same thing, medicine with gymnastic and justice with the legislative art; on the other hand, they nevertheless differ somewhat from each other. Now these are four, and always take care—some of the body, the others of the soul—in accord with what is best. But flattery[43] perceived this (I do not mean by knowing but by guessing), divided itself into four, and slipped in under each of the

464d parts; it pretends to be this that it has slipped in under, and gives no heed to the best but hunts after folly with what is ever most pleasant,

---

42. Reading *dikaiosunē*; an alternate reading, *dikastikē*, could be translated "the judge's art," as at 520b.

43. Socrates uses feminine singular *kolakeutikē*; were it not for the context, my usual practice would lead me to translate "the art of flattery."

and deceives, so as to seem to be worth very much. So cookery has slipped in under medicine and pretends to know the best foods for the body, so that, if the cook and the doctor had to contest among children or among men as thoughtless as children which of the two, 464e the doctor or the cook, has understanding about useful and bad foods, the doctor would die of hunger. This, therefore, I call flattery, 465a and I assert that such a thing is shameful, Polus—for I am saying this to you—because it guesses at the pleasant without the best. And I assert that it is not art but experience, because it has no reasoned account, in regard to the thing to which it administers or the things that it administers, of what sort of things they are in their nature; and so it cannot state the cause of each thing. And I do not call art, a business that lacks a reasoned account. But if you disagree about these things, I am willing to provide a reasoned account.

465b   Beneath medicine, therefore, as I'm saying, lies the flattery of cookery; and beneath gymnastic, according to this same manner, lies cosmetic, in that it is evildoing, deceitful, ignoble, and unfree, deceiving with shapes, colors, smoothness, and garments, so as to make them, as they take upon themselves an alien beauty, neglect their own beauty that comes through gymnastic. So in order not to speak at length, I want to speak to you just as the geometers do—for perhaps 465c you are already following me—saying that as cosmetic is to gymnastic, so is cookery to medicine; or rather thus: as cosmetic is to gymnastic, so is sophistry to the legislative art; and as cookery is to medicine, so is rhetoric to justice. As I was saying, however, this is the way they differ by nature, but—inasmuch as they are closely related —sophists and rhetors are mixed together in the same place and about the same things, and they do not know what use to make of themselves nor do other human beings know what use to make of them. 465d For indeed if the soul were not set over the body, but the body were set over itself, and if cookery and medicine were not contemplated and distinguished by the soul, but the body itself decided, measuring by the gratifications for itself, the saying of Anaxagoras[44] would be much to the point, Polus my friend—for you are experienced in these

44. The pre-Socratic philosopher Anaxagoras appears to have taught that some amount of each material is present in every thing. Socrates names him as a crucial influence on Pericles at *Phaedrus* 270a and quotes this same saying in *Phaedo* 72c. When Meletus says that Socrates teaches that the sun is a stone and the moon earth, Socrates belittles the accusation by asking Meletus whether he thinks he is accusing Anaxagoras (*Apology* 26d). In his brief

things—all matters would be mixed up together in the same place, with the things of medicine, health, and cookery indistinguishable.

So then, you have heard what I say rhetoric is: the counterpart of cookery in the soul, as that [is the counterpart of rhetoric] in the body.

465e Perhaps, then, I have done a strange thing in that, not permitting you to make lengthy speeches, I have myself extended a long speech. It is then appropriate to pardon me; for when I spoke briefly, you did not understand, and you were able to make no use of the answer that I gave you, but needed a full description. So then, when you are an-

466a swering, if I too do not know what use to make of it, you too extend your speech; but if I do, let me make use of it; for that is just. And now, if you can make some use of this answer, do so.

POL.: What then are you saying? Does rhetoric seem to you to be flattery?

SOC.: Nay rather I said a part of flattery. But do you not remember at your age, Polus? What will you do later?

POL.: So, do good rhetors therefore seem to you to be esteemed as lowly flatterers in the cities?

SOC.: Do you ask this as a question or are you stating the beginning

466b of some speech?

POL.: I am asking.

SOC.: In my opinion, at any rate, they are not even esteemed.

POL.: What do you mean, not esteemed? Do they not have the greatest power in the cities?

SOC.: No, at least if you say that having power is something good for him who has it.

POL.: Indeed, I certainly do say so.

SOC.: Well then, rhetors seem to me to have the least power of those in the city.

POL.: What's this? Do they not, just like tyrants, kill whomever they

466c wish, and confiscate possessions, and expel from the cities whomever it seems good to them[45]?

SOC.: By the dog, I am certainly of two minds, Polus, on each thing you say, whether you yourself are saying these things and revealing your own opinion, or whether you are asking me.

intellectual autobiography (*Phaedo* 97b–98c), Socrates recounts his intense interest, followed by disappointment, in Anaxagoras.

45. This phrase is regularly used for resolutions of the council and assembly in Athens; more literally it says, simply, "it seems to them."

POL.: Well, I am asking you.

SOC.: So be it, my friend. In that case are you asking me two things at once?

POL.: How so, two things?

SOC.: Were you not just now saying something like this: "Do not rhe-
466d tors kill those whom they wish, just like tyrants, and confiscate possessions and drive out of the cities whomever it seems good to them?"

POL.: I was.

SOC.: Well then, I say to you that these are two questions, and I shall
answer you both of them. For I assert, Polus, that both rhetors and
tyrants have the smallest power in the cities, as I was saying just now;
466e for they do nothing, one might almost say, of what they wish, although they certainly do what seems to them to be best.

POL.: Is not this, then, having great power?

SOC.: No, at least not as Polus says.

POL.: I say not? But I do indeed say so!

SOC.: By the . . . ! You do not, since you say that having great power
is good for the one who has it.

POL.: I do indeed say so.

SOC.: Do you then think it is good, if someone who does not have intelligence does those things that seem to him to be best? And do you
call this having great power?

POL.: No, I don't.

SOC.: Will you therefore show that rhetors have intelligence and that
467a rhetoric is an art, but not flattery, having refuted me? If you leave me
unrefuted, rhetors who do what seems good to them in the cities and
tyrants will have acquired nothing good by this. And power is, as
you say, a good thing, but you too agree that doing what seems good
without intelligence is a bad thing; don't you?

POL.: I do.

SOC.: How then would rhetors or tyrants have great power in the
cities, unless Socrates is refuted by Polus, to the effect that they do
what they wish?

467b POL.: This man here . . . !

SOC.: I deny that they do what they wish. Well, refute me!

POL.: Weren't you just now agreeing that they do what seems to them
to be best?

SOC.: Yes, and I agree now too.

POL.: So do they not then do what they wish?

soc.: I say not.

pol.: Doing what seems good to them?

soc.: Yes, I say.

pol.: You are saying shocking and extraordinary things, Socrates.

soc.: Don't be an accuser, most agreeable Polus—to address you af-
467c   ter your fashion.[46] But if you have something to ask me, show that I
am speaking false, and if not, answer yourself.

pol.: Well, I am willing to answer, so that I may know what you're
saying.

soc.: Do human beings then seem to you to wish what they do on
each occasion, or that for the sake of which they do what they do?
For example, do those who drink a drug from the doctors seem to
you to wish this thing that they are doing, drinking the drug and
suffering pain, or that thing, being healthy, for the sake of which they
drink?

467d   pol.: Being healthy, clearly.

soc.: So then, both those who sail and those who transact other moneymaking business: what they wish is not what they do on each occasion (for who wishes to sail and be in danger and have troubles?)
but, I think, that for the sake of which they sail, being wealthy; for
they sail for the sake of wealth.

pol.: Certainly.

soc.: So isn't it also this way concerning all things? Whenever someone does something for the sake of something, he doesn't wish what
467e   he does, but that for the sake of which he does it?

pol.: Yes.

soc.: Now, among the things that are, is there anything that is neither
good nor bad nor between these (neither good nor bad)?

pol.: No, very necessarily, Socrates.

soc.: So then, do you say that wisdom and health and wealth and the
other such things are good, and the opposites of these are bad?

pol.: I do.

soc.: Do you therefore say that things neither good nor bad are such
as sometimes have a share in the good, sometimes in the bad, and
468a   sometimes in neither, such as sitting, walking, running, and sailing,

---

46. Many editors prefer the correction "Don't speak evil." "Most agreeable Polus" is *ō lōiste
Pōle*, with a jingling assonance that caricatures Polus's and Gorgias's rhetorical devices.
Lamb's "peerless Polus" hits the mark (W. R. M. Lamb, *Plato V; Lysis Symposium Gorgias*,
Loeb Library [Cambridge: Harvard University Press, 1925]), p. 327.

and again stones, wood, and the other such things? Don't you say these things? Or do you call some other things neither good nor bad?

POL.: No, these things.

SOC.: Well then, do they do these in-between things, whenever they do them, for the sake of the good ones, or the good things for the sake of the in-between ones?

468b   POL.: The in-between things, doubtless, for the sake of the good ones.

SOC.: It is therefore in pursuit of the good that we walk whenever we walk, thinking it to be better; and, the opposite, that we stand still whenever we stand still, for the sake of the same thing, the good; isn't it?

POL.: Yes.

SOC.: So then do we also kill, if we kill someone, and expel and con- fiscate possessions, thinking it is better for us to do these things than not?

POL.: Certainly.

SOC.: Those who do all these things, therefore, do them for the sake of the good.

POL.: I say so.

SOC.: Have we then agreed that we do not wish those things that we do for the sake of something, but that thing for the sake of which we

468c   do these things?

POL.: Very much so.

SOC.: We therefore do not wish to slaughter or to expel from the cities or to confiscate possessions simply like that; but when these things are beneficial for us, we wish to do them, and we do not wish them when harmful. For we wish the good things, as you say, but we do not wish the things that are neither good nor bad, nor the bad things. Isn't that so? Does what I'm saying seem true to you Polus, or not? Why do you not answer?

POL.: True.

468d   SOC.: If we agree on these things, then, if someone kills someone or ex- pels him from the city or confiscates possessions, whether he is a tyrant or a rhetor, thinking this to be better for himself, but it happens to be worse, this man doubtless does what seems good to him; doesn't he?

POL.: Yes.

SOC.: Well then, does he therefore also do what he wishes, if these things happen to be bad? Why do you not answer?

POL.: Well, he does not seem to me to do what he wishes.

soc.: So then, is there some way in which such a one has great power
468e   in that city, if indeed having great power is something good, according to your agreement?

pol.: There is not.

soc.: What I was saying is therefore true, when I said that it is possible for a human being who does in the city what seems good to him
not to have great power nor to do what he wishes.

pol.: As if indeed you, Socrates, would not welcome the possibility
of your doing what seemed good to you in the city, rather than not,
and would not feel envy when you see someone killing whomever it
seemed good to him or confiscating possessions or putting him in
fetters.

soc.: Do you mean justly or unjustly?

469a   pol.: Whichever he does, is it not enviable either way?

soc.: Hush, Polus![47]

pol.: Why so?

soc.: Because one must not envy either the unenviable or the
wretched, but pity them.

pol.: How so? Do the human beings that I am speaking about seem
to you to be in such a condition?

soc.: How could they not?

pol.: So then when someone kills whomever it seems good to him,
killing justly, does he seem to you to be wretched and pitiable?

soc.: No, not to me at least; but not enviable either.

pol.: Didn't you just say he was wretched?

469b   soc.: That is the one who killed unjustly, comrade, and he is pitiable
to boot; the one who kills justly is unenviable.

pol.: Surely the one who is put to death unjustly, at any rate, is
pitiable and wretched, I suppose.

soc.: Less than he who kills, Polus, and less than he who is justly put
to death.

pol.: How is this, Socrates?

soc.: In this way, that doing injustice happens to be the greatest of
evils.

pol.: Can it be that this is the greatest? Isn't suffering injustice greater?

soc.: Not in the least.

---

47. *Euphēmei:* to avoid unlucky words, to keep a religious silence; the opposite of to blas-
pheme.

POL.: Would you then wish to suffer injustice rather than to do injustice?

469c   SOC.: I for one would wish neither; but if it were necessary to do or to suffer injustice, I would choose rather to suffer than to do injustice.

POL.: You would therefore not welcome ruling as tyrant?

SOC.: No, at least not if by ruling as tyrant you mean what I do.

POL.: Well, I mean this same thing as just now: the possibility of doing in the city whatever seems good to oneself, killing and expelling and doing all things in accord with one's opinion.

SOC.: Blessed one, as I now speak, you go ahead and raise objections.

469d   If in the crowded marketplace I took a dagger from under my arm and said to you, "Polus, a certain power and an amazing tyranny have just now accrued to me. For if indeed it seems good to me that someone of these human beings that you see must straightaway die, this one shall die, as seems good to me. And if it seems good to me that one of them must have his head smashed, it shall straightaway

469e   be smashed; and if his cloak must be torn, it shall be torn. Such great power do I have in this city." If then you distrusted me and I showed you the dagger, upon seeing it you might perhaps say, "Socrates, in this way all people would have great power, since any house that seemed good to you would be burned in this fashion, and the Athenians' dockyards and triremes and all the ships and things public and private." But therefore having great power is not this: to do what seems good to oneself; or does it seem so to you?

POL.: Indeed not—not in this way, at least.

470a   SOC.: Can you then say for what reason you blame such power?

POL.: I can.

SOC.: What is it then? Speak!

POL.: Because it is necessary for someone who acts in this manner to pay a penalty.

SOC.: And isn't paying a penalty a bad thing?

POL.: Certainly.

SOC.: So then, you amazing man, it comes back again to light for you that if acting beneficially accompanies the one who does what seems good, it's a good thing, and this, as it seems, is having great power;

470b   but if not, it's a bad thing, and having small power. And let us examine this too: don't we agree that sometimes it's better to do those things we were just now speaking of, to kill and drive human beings out and confiscate possessions, but sometimes not?

POL.: Certainly.

SOC.: This, then, as it seems, is agreed on both by you and by me.

POL.: Yes.

SOC.: When, therefore, do you say it is better to do those things? Say what boundary you define.

POL.: Really now, Socrates, you answer this.

470c   SOC.: I do indeed assert then, Polus—if it is more pleasant for you to hear from me—that when someone does those things justly, it is better, but when unjustly, worse.

POL.: It's really hard to refute you, Socrates. But would not even a child refute you, and show that what you're saying isn't true?

SOC.: I shall feel much gratitude to the child then, and equal gratitude to you too, if you refute me and release me from drivel. So don't tire of doing good to a man who's a friend, but refute.

POL.: Very well then, Socrates, there's no need to refute you with an-
470d   cient affairs; for these things that happened just yesterday or the day before are sufficient to refute you and to show that many human beings who do injustice are happy.

SOC.: What sort of things are these?

POL.: You see, I suppose, that that fellow Archelaus[48] the son of Perdiccas rules Macedonia?

SOC.: If not, at least I hear so.

POL.: Well then, does he seem to you to be happy or wretched?

SOC.: I don't know, Polus; for I have not yet been with the man.

470e   POL.: What? You would know if you were with him, but otherwise, on the spot, you do not know that he is happy?

SOC.: By Zeus, indeed I do not.

POL.: It's clear then, Socrates, that you will say you don't know that the great king[49] is happy either.

---

48. Archelaus ruled Macedonia from 413 to 399, dying the same year as Socrates. Dodds notes: "Leading poets like Euripides [and] Agathon . . . had accepted his hospitality, exchanging the miseries of war-time Athens for what Aristophanes called 'the fleshpots of the Happy Land' (. . . *Frogs* 85)." Gorgias may also have spent time at his court; Aristotle (*Rhetoric* 1398a) reports that Socrates refused the invitation. Thucydides (2.100.2) reports on Archelaus's building of roads and fortresses and his arranging military forces and equipment stronger than what all the eight previous kings of Macedonia had done; in this respect he bears an important resemblance to Athenian imperial statesmen criticized by Socrates later in this dialogue.

49. The great king, that is, of Persia, is proverbial among Greeks for someone happy according to the most common criteria; see, for example, *Apology of Socrates* 40d–e.

soc.: And what I'll say is true; for I do not know how he stands in regard to education and justice.

pol.: What? Is the whole of happiness in this?

soc.: As I say, at any rate, Polus. For I assert that the noble and good[50]
man and woman are happy; the unjust and base, wretched.

471a pol.: Then is this Archelaus wretched according to your argument?

soc.: If indeed, my friend, he is unjust.

pol.: But how on earth could he not be unjust? No part of the rule
that he now has belongs to him at all, since he was born of a woman
who was the slave of Alcetas, Perdiccas's brother, and in accordance
with the just he was Alcetas's slave; and if he wished to do the just
things, he would be a slave to Alcetas and would be happy, according to your argument. But now, how amazingly wretched he has be-
471b come, since he has done the greatest unjust deeds! First, he sent for
this man, his very master and uncle, as if he was going to give back
the rule that Perdiccas had taken away from him; having entertained
him and his son Alexander (his own first cousin, of about the same
age) as guests and got them drunk, he threw them into a wagon and,
dragging them away by night, cut their throats and did away with
them both. And having done these unjust things, it escaped his notice that he had become most wretched, and he did not repent. But a
471c little later he did not wish to become happy by justly rearing and giving back the rule to his brother, the legitimate son of Perdiccas, a child
about seven years old, to whom the rule passed in accordance with
the just; but he threw him into a well and drowned him, and told the
child's mother, Cleopatra, that he had fallen in and died while chas-
ing a goose. So therefore now, seeing that he has done the greatest
unjust deeds in Macedonia, he is the most wretched of all Macedonians, not the most happy; and perhaps there is some one of the Athe-
471d nians, starting with you, who would welcome becoming anybody
else whatsoever of the Macedonians rather than Archelaus.

soc.: Toward the beginning of the speeches, Polus, I praised you in
that you seem to me to have been well educated in regard to rhetoric—but I said you have neglected conversing. And now is this the
speech by which even a child would refute me? And have I now, as

---

50. *Kalos kagathos* is a standard formula for something like "the complete gentleman"; the
term was also used by the aristocratic party to distinguish themselves from common folk.
Dodds notes that he has nowhere else found the phrase applied to women.

you think, been refuted by you through this speech, I who affirm that the one who does injustice is not happy? How can it possibly be, good fellow? On the contrary, I certainly do not agree with you on any one of these things that you are asserting.

471e   POL.: No, for you do not want to, since it seems to you as I say.

soc.: You blessed one, you are now attempting to refute me rhetorically, just like those who think they are refuting in the law courts. For in that place, the ones seem to refute the others, when they provide many witnesses of good repute for the speeches that they make, while he who says the opposite provides some one witness or none.

472a   But this refutation is worth nothing in regard to the truth; for on some occasions someone would be borne down by the false witness of many who seem to be something. And now concerning the things you are saying, all Athenians and foreigners, save a few, will assert the same things along with you, if you wish to provide witnesses against me to testify that what I'm saying isn't true. Nicias the son of Niceratus and his brothers with him, whose tripods are standing in a row in the precinct of Dionysus, will bear witness for you, if you

472b   wish; and if you wish, Aristocrates the son of Scellias, whose beautiful votive offering in turn this is in the precinct of Pythian Apollo; and if you wish, the whole house of Pericles or whatever other family you wish to pick out from the inhabitants here.[51] But I, being one man, do not agree with you. For you do not compel me, but, providing many false witnesses against me, you are attempting to expel me from my substance and the truth. But if I do not provide you yourself, being one man, as the witness in agreement with the things I'm saying, I think I have accomplished nothing worth speaking of con-

472c   cerning the things that our argument is about; nor, I think, have you, unless I, being one man alone, bear witness for you, and you bid all these others farewell. So then, there is this certain manner of refutation, as you and many others think; and there is another, which I, in

---

51. The witnesses Socrates imagines cover the whole Athenian political spectrum. Pericles and his family (including his nephew Alcibiades) were leaders of the democratic (to some, extreme democratic) party in Athens. Aristocrates was oligarchic (mentioned by Thucydides, 8.89.2, as a member of the oligarchic government of the Four Hundred after the defeat of Athens's Sicilian expedition). Nicias was a moderate: wealthy, of conservative bent, and loyal to the democracy, as were his brothers (Lysias 18.4–12); Nicias's views on education and virtue, as depicted by Plato, may be found in the *Laches*. The sacred offerings of Nicias and Aristocrates evoke their wealth and high standing in the community; no such evidence is cited, perhaps because not needed, regarding Pericles.

turn, think should be. So, having put them beside each other, let us then consider if they differ in some respect from each other. For indeed these things that we are disagreeing about do not happen to be at all small, but are more or less those things that it is most fine to know about and most shameful not to know about; for the chief point of them is either to know or to ignore who is happy and who is

472d not. The immediately first thing, that our argument now is about: you think that a man who does injustice and is unjust can be blessed, if indeed you think that Archelaus is unjust but happy. Should we not understand you to have such a belief?

POL.: Certainly.

SOC.: But I say it's impossible. This indeed is one thing we disagree on. So be it; the doer of injustice, then, will be happy; will this be so, then, if he meets with just judgment and retribution?

POL.: Not in the least, since thus he would be most wretched.

472e SOC.: But if, then, the doer of injustice does not meet with just judgment, according to your argument he will be happy.

POL.: So I assert.

SOC.: But according to my opinion, at least, Polus, the one who does injustice and is unjust is altogether wretched, but more wretched if he does not pay the just penalty nor meet with retribution when he does injustice, and less wretched if he pays the just penalty and meets with just judgment from gods and human beings.

473a POL.: You are attempting to say strange things indeed, Socrates.

SOC.: And I shall try, at least, to make you too, comrade, say the same things to me: for I consider you a friend. Well now, these then are the things on which we differ; and you consider them too. I was saying earlier, I suppose, that doing injustice is worse than suffering injustice.

POL.: Certainly.

SOC.: But you said suffering injustice is worse.

POL.: Yes.

SOC.: And I asserted that the doers of injustice are wretched, and I was refuted by you.

POL.: Yes, by Zeus!

SOC.: As you think, Polus.

473b POL.: And what I think is true.

SOC.: Perhaps. But you in turn say that the doers of injustice are happy, if they do not pay the just penalty.

POL.: Yes, certainly.

soc.: But I assert that they are most wretched, but those who pay the just penalty are less so. Do you wish to refute this too?

pol.: Well, this is still harder to refute, Socrates, than that.

soc.: Not so, to be sure, Polus, but rather impossible: for what is true is never refuted.

pol.: What do you mean? If someone is caught doing injustice, plot-
473c ting to attain tyranny, and having been caught is tortured on the rack and castrated and has his eyes burned out, and having suffered many great mutilations of all kinds himself and having beheld his children and wife suffer them, at the end is impaled or tarred and burned—this man will be happier than if, getting away, he is estab-lished as tyrant, rules in the city, and passes his whole life doing whatever he wishes, being enviable and accounted happy by the cit-
473d izens and by others who are foreigners? These are the things you say it is impossible to refute?

soc.: Now in turn you are frightening us with bogeymen, nobly born Polus, and not refuting; and a moment ago you were calling wit-nesses. But remind me nevertheless of a little thing. Did you say, if he unjustly plots to attain tyranny?

pol.: I did.

soc.: Then surely neither one of them shall ever be happier, neither the one who has unjustly achieved tyranny nor the one who pays the just penalty—for of two wretched men, one would not be happier—but the one who gets away and becomes tyrant is nevertheless more
473e wretched. What's this, Polus? Are you laughing? Is this yet another form of refutation—when someone says something, to laugh it down and not to refute?

pol.: Do you not think you have been refuted, Socrates, when you say such things as no one among human beings would assert? Just ask anyone of these men.

soc.: Polus, I am not one of the political men,[52] and when last year I was by lot a member of the council and my tribe was presiding and I had to put a question to the vote, I gave people a laugh and didn't
474a know how to put it to the vote.[53] So then, now too do not bid me to

52. *Politikoi*: statesmen, politicians, men skilled in politics. At *Apology* 32a–c, Socrates jux-taposes his not holding political office with his service on the council and his consequent role in the trial of the generals at Arginusae in 406.

53. Most scholars, including Dodds on 473e7, consider this to be a self-deprecating reference to Socrates' opposition to the condemnation of the generals in 406. They had won a naval

put the vote to those present, but if you do not have a better refutation than these things, as I was just now saying, give the refutation over to me in my turn, and make trial of the sort of refutation that I think ought to be. For I know how to provide one witness for what I say, the man himself to whom my speech is directed, while I bid the many farewell; and I know how to put the vote to one man, while I
474b don't converse with the many either. See then if you'll be willing in your turn to give occasion for refutation, by answering the things asked. For surely I think that I and you and the other human beings consider doing injustice worse than suffering injustice, and not paying the just penalty worse than paying it.

POL.: But I, for one, think that neither I nor any other human being does. So you would welcome suffering injustice rather than doing injustice?

SOC.: And so would you, and all others.

POL.: Far from it—not I nor you nor anyone else!

474c SOC.: So then, will you answer?

POL.: Yes, certainly; for I desire to know what on earth you'll say.

SOC.: Now then tell me, in order that you may know, as if I were asking you from the beginning. Which seems to you, Polus, to be worse, doing injustice or suffering injustice?

POL.: Suffering injustice, as far as I'm concerned.

SOC.: And now what about this? Which is more shameful, doing injustice or suffering injustice? Answer!

POL.: Doing injustice.

SOC.: So then it is also worse, if indeed it is more shameful.

POL.: Not in the least.

SOC.: I understand; it looks as though you do not consider fine and
474d good, and bad and shameful, to be the same thing.

POL.: Indeed not.

SOC.: And what about this? All fine things, such as bodies, colors, shapes, voices, and practices—do you call them fine on each occasion without looking toward anything? First, for example, don't you say that beautiful bodies are beautiful either in reference to the use, for

---

battle but were accused of failure to gather up the bodies of the dead. Socrates opposed their being tried en masse as illegal, and was the only one of the Pyrtaneis (executive or presiding committee) to stand by this position despite the threats of the rhetors and the anger of the multitude. The fullest account is in Xenophon's *Hellenica* 1.7 (which does not assert, however, that Socrates was individually in the position to put the question to the vote).

this thing that each is useful for, or in reference to some pleasure, if it makes those who look upon it rejoice in the looking? Do you have anything beyond these things to say about the beauty of the body?

474e   POL.: No, I don't.

SOC.: So then, is it this way with all the other things too, and do you call both shapes and colors beautiful on account of some pleasure or benefit or both?

POL.: I do.

SOC.: And isn't it the same with voices and all things relating to music?

POL.: Yes.

SOC.: And indeed for things relating to laws and practices—fine ones, that is—doubtless there isn't anything beyond these: their being either beneficial or pleasant or both.

475a   POL.: Not in my opinion, at any rate.

SOC.: So then, is it also the same with the beauty of sciences?

POL.: Certainly; and you are giving a fine definition now, Socrates, when you define the fine by pleasure and goodness.[54]

SOC.: So then the shameful is defined by the opposite, by pain and badness?

POL.: Necessarily.

SOC.: Whenever, therefore, one of two fine things is finer, it is finer by surpassing in one of these two things or both, either in pleasure or in benefit or in both.

POL.: Certainly.

SOC.: And then whenever one of two shameful things is more shame-
475b   ful, it will be more shameful by surpassing in either pain or badness. Or isn't that necessary?

POL.: Yes.

SOC.: Come then, what was being said just now about doing injustice and suffering injustice? Weren't you saying that suffering injustice is worse, but doing injustice is more shameful?

POL.: I was.

SOC.: So then, if doing injustice is more shameful than suffering injustice, either it is more painful and would be more shameful by surpassing in pain, or in badness, or in both. Isn't this also necessary?

54. In the *Hippias Major*, Socrates investigates just what the fine (noble, beautiful) is; it proves very difficult to state.

POL.: How could it not be?

475c   SOC.: Now first let us consider this: does doing injustice therefore surpass suffering injustice in pain, and do the doers of injustice feel more pain than the sufferers of injustice?

POL.: Surely this, Socrates, is not at all the case.

SOC.: Therefore it does not exceed in pain.

POL.: Indeed not.

SOC.: So then if not in pain, it would further not surpass in both.

POL.: It appears not.

SOC.: So what remains then is surpassing in the other.

POL.: Yes.

SOC.: In badness.

POL.: It looks that way.

SOC.: So then, by surpassing in badness, doing injustice would be worse than suffering injustice.

POL.: That's clear now.

475d   SOC.: Now then, don't the great majority of human beings agree, and didn't you agree with us at the earlier time, that doing injustice is more shameful than suffering injustice?

POL.: Yes.

SOC.: And now, at any rate, it has come to light as worse.

POL.: It looks that way.

SOC.: Would you then welcome the worse and the more shameful rather than what is less so? Don't shrink from answering, Polus; for you will suffer no harm. But submit yourself in a nobly born manner to the argument as to a doctor, and answer. Say either yes or no to

475e   what I'm asking.

POL.: Well, I would not welcome it, Socrates.

SOC.: And would any other human being?

POL.: It doesn't seem so to me, at least according to this argument.

SOC.: What I was saying was therefore true, that neither I nor you nor any other human being would welcome doing injustice rather than suffering injustice; for it happens to be worse.

POL.: So it appears.

SOC.: So you see then, Polus, that when one refutation is put beside the other, they don't look like each other at all; but all other men agree with you except me, whereas for me you, being one man alone,

476a   are quite enough both to agree and to bear witness, and I put the vote to you alone and bid the others farewell. And let this matter stand thus with us. Now after this, let us consider the second thing that we disagreed about: whether it is the greatest of evils for the doer of injustice to pay the just penalty, as you thought, or whether not paying is a greater evil, as I in turn thought. Let's examine it this way: do you call it the same thing, then, for the doer of injustice to pay the just penalty and to be punished[55] justly?

POL.: I do.

476b   SOC.: Now then, can you say that not all just things are fine, insofar as they are just? And speak when you have examined it thoroughly.

POL.: Well, they seem so to me, Socrates.

SOC.: Now consider this too: if someone does something, must there necessarily also be something that suffers from this one who is doing it?

POL.: It seems so to me, at least.

SOC.: So does this thing suffer what the doer does and suffer the sort of thing that the doer does? I mean something of the following sort: if someone beats, is it necessary that something is beaten?

POL.: Necessarily.

476c   SOC.: And if the beater beats violently or rapidly, must what is beaten be beaten in this way too?

POL.: Yes.

SOC.: Is the passive condition of what is beaten, therefore, such as what the beater does?

POL.: Certainly.

SOC.: So then too, if someone burns, is it necessary that something be burned?

POL.: How could it not be?

SOC.: And if it burns violently or painfully, is what is burned burned in the same way as the burner burns?

POL.: Certainly.

SOC.: So then too, if someone cuts, does the same argument hold? For something is cut.

POL.: Yes.

SOC.: And if the cut is big or deep or painful, is what is cut cut with
476d   such a cut as the cutter cuts?

POL.: It appears so.

---

55. *Kolazein:* to check, correct, chastise, punish. Aristotle notes that people are trained to avoid *akolasia* (intemperance, licentiousness, immoderation) through having their desires chastened, beginning in childhood (*Nicomachean Ethics* 1119a34–b15).

soc.: In sum, now, see if you agree on what I was recently saying, concerning all things: that which suffers suffers such a thing as what the doer does.

pol.: Well, I agree.

soc.: These things now being agreed on, is paying the just penalty suffering something or doing something?

pol.: Of necessity, Socrates, it is suffering.

soc.: Then is it from someone doing it?

pol.: How could it not be? It is from him who punishes.

476e   soc.: And does he who punishes correctly punish justly?

pol.: Yes.

soc.: Doing just things, or not?

pol.: Just things.

soc.: So then does he who is punished and pays the just penalty suffer just things?

pol.: It appears so.

soc.: And it's been agreed, I suppose, that just things are fine?

pol.: Certainly.

soc.: Of these men, therefore, the one does fine things, and the other, the one punished, suffers them.

pol.: Yes.

477a   soc.: So if fine, then good? For they are either pleasant or beneficial.

pol.: Necessarily.

soc.: He who pays the just penalty therefore suffers good things?

pol.: It looks like it.

soc.: He is therefore benefited?

pol.: Yes.

soc.: Then what do I suppose the benefit to be? Does he become better in respect to his soul, if he is justly punished?

pol.: That's likely.

soc.: Is he who pays the just penalty therefore released from badness of soul?

pol.: Yes.

477b   soc.: So is he therefore released from the greatest evil? Consider it this way: do you see any other badness in the constitution of a human being's possessions than poverty?

pol.: No, just poverty.

soc.: And how about in the body's constitution? Would you say badness is weakness, sickness, ugliness, and such things?

POL.: I would.

SOC.: So then, do you think there is any baseness in soul too?

POL.: How could I not?

SOC.: Don't you call this injustice, lack of learning, cowardice, and such things?

POL.: Yes, certainly.

477c SOC.: So then, of possessions and body and soul, which are three, have you stated threefold kinds of baseness: poverty, sickness, and injustice?

POL.: Yes.

SOC.: Which of these kinds of baseness, then, is most shameful? Is it not injustice and, in sum, the soul's baseness?

POL.: Very much so.

SOC.: If most shameful, then also worst?

POL.: How do you mean it, Socrates?

SOC.: In this way: what is ever most shameful is most shameful by providing the greatest pain or harm or both, on the basis of the things agreed on earlier.

POL.: Most certainly.

SOC.: And have we just now agreed that the most shameful thing is
477d injustice and the whole baseness of soul?

POL.: Yes, we agreed.

SOC.: So then is it either most painful and is the most shameful of these by surpassing in painfulness, or in harm, or both?

POL.: Necessarily.

SOC.: Well then, is being unjust, intemperate, cowardly, and un-learned more painful than being poor and being sick?

POL.: It doesn't seem so to me, Socrates, at least not on the basis of these things.

SOC.: It is therefore by surpassing the others in some extraordinarily great harm and amazing evil that baseness of soul is most shameful
477e of all, since it is not in painfulness, at any rate, as your argument goes.

POL.: It appears so.

SOC.: But surely, I suppose, what surpasses in the greatest harm would be the greatest evil among the things that are.

POL.: Yes.

SOC.: Are injustice and intemperance and the other baseness of soul therefore the greatest evil among the things that are?

POL.: It appears so.

soc.: Now then, what art releases one from poverty? Isn't it money-making?

pol.: Yes.

soc.: And what art releases one from sickness? Isn't it medicine?

478a pol.: Necessarily.

soc.: And what art releases one from baseness and injustice? If you're not well-supplied with answers just like that, consider it this way: where, and to what people, do we lead those who are sick in their bodies?

pol.: To doctors, Socrates.

soc.: And where do we lead those who do injustice and are intemperate?

pol.: Do you mean, to judges?

soc.: Is it so that they will pay the just penalty?

pol.: I say so.

soc.: Now then, don't those who punish correctly punish by using a certain justice?

pol.: That's clear, surely.

478b soc.: Moneymaking therefore releases one from poverty, medicine from sickness, and justice[56] from intemperance and injustice.

pol.: So it appears.

soc.: Which of these things, then, is finest?

pol.: What things do you mean?

soc.: Moneymaking, medicine, justice.

pol.: Justice, Socrates, excels by much.

soc.: So then, again, does it produce the most pleasure or benefit or both, if indeed it is finest?

pol.: Yes.

soc.: Well then, is it pleasant to be medically treated, and do those who are medically treated rejoice?

pol.: Not in my opinion, at least.

soc.: But it's beneficial, at any rate, isn't it?

---

56. Here, *dikē*, the root form (in other usages, I have translated it "just judgment" and "just penalty"). Usually, "justice" translates *dikaiosunē*. The unexplained variation in the terms Socrates uses relating to justice reminds us that his refutation of Polus turns on what sort of thing justice is (or more precisely, what sorts of things doing and suffering injustice are) without specifying what justice is—a rhetorical offense against conversing of which he accused Polus at 448e.

478c   POL.: Yes.

SOC.: For he is released from a great evil, so that it is profitable to endure the pain and be healthy.

POL.: How could it not be?

SOC.: So in this way, then, would the happiest human being in respect to the body be he who is medically treated, or he who is not even sick in the first place?

POL.: He who is not even sick, clearly.

SOC.: Then it looks as though happiness was not this, the release from evil, but not even acquiring it in the first place.

POL.: That is so.

478d   SOC.: And what about this? Of two men who have an evil either in body or in soul, which is more wretched, the one who is medically treated and released from the evil, or the one who is not medically treated and has it?

POL.: As it appears to me, the one who is not medically treated.

SOC.: So then, was paying the just penalty the release from the greatest evil, baseness?

POL.: It was indeed.

SOC.: For justice doubtless moderates men and makes them more just and comes to be the medicine for baseness.

POL.: Yes.

SOC.: Happiest, therefore, is he who does not have badness in his soul,
478e   since this came to light as the greatest of evils.

POL.: Yes, clearly.

SOC.: And second, doubtless, is he who is released from it.

POL.: It looks that way.

SOC.: And this was the man who is admonished, is rebuked, and pays the just penalty.

POL.: Yes.

SOC.: Therefore he lives worst who has injustice[57] and is not released from it.

POL.: So it appears.

SOC.: So does this then happen to be he who, doing the greatest unjust deeds and making use of the greatest injustice, brings it about

---

57. Some editors consider "injustice" probably a gloss because it anticipates the next step in the argument; if so, one should drop it and understand "badness" as the object of "has."

479a   that he is neither admonished nor punished nor pays the just penalty, just as you assert Archelaus has managed to do, and the other tyrants and rhetors and potentates?[58]

POL.: It looks that way.

SOC.: For doubtless these men have brought about approximately the same thing, you best of men, as if some one afflicted with the greatest sicknesses brought it about that he not pay the just penalty for the errors concerning his body to the doctors and not be medically treated, fearing, as if he were a child, the burning and cutting, because it's

479b   painful. Or doesn't it seem so to you too?

POL.: It does to me.

SOC.: Through ignoring, as it would appear, what sort of thing health and virtue of body are. And indeed from what we have now agreed on, those too who flee justice run the risk of doing something of the same sort, Polus: observing its painfulness, but being blind to its beneficial quality and ignoring how much more wretched a thing than an unhealthy body it is to dwell with a soul that is not healthy but

479c   rotten, unjust, and impious; whence they also do everything so as not to pay the just penalty or be released from the greatest evil, preparing for themselves possessions and friends and that they themselves should be as persuasive as possible in speaking. And if the things we have agreed on are true, Polus, do you then perceive the implications of the argument? Or do you wish that we sum them up?

POL.: If it seems good to you in any case.

SOC.: So then, does it follow that injustice and doing injustice are the

479d   greatest evil?

POL.: It appears so, at any rate.

SOC.: And surely paying the just penalty came to light as the release from this evil?

POL.: It may be.

SOC.: But not paying is abiding in the evil?

POL.: Yes.

SOC.: Then doing injustice is second among the evils in greatness; and for the doer of injustice not to pay the just penalty is naturally the greatest and first of all evils.

---

58. A *dunastēs* is one of a small number who collectively rule in a tyrannical manner; a *dunasteia* (see 492b) could be called a narrow arbitrary oligarchy or a junta. The term was used to describe the Thirty Tyrants brought to power with Spartan support at the end of

POL.: It looks that way.

SOC.: So then, was it not about this, my friend, that we disagreed? You accounted Archelaus happy for doing the greatest unjust deeds with-

479e out paying any just penalty, whereas I thought the opposite, that if either Archelaus or any other human being whatsoever did not pay the just penalty when he did injustice, it properly belonged to him to be preeminently wretched among other human beings, and that he who does injustice is always more wretched than he who suffers injustice, and he who does not pay the just penalty is more wretched than he who pays. Weren't these the things that I said?

POL.: Yes.

SOC.: So then has it been proved that they were truly said?

POL.: It appears so.

480a SOC.: So be it. Now then, if these things are true, Polus, what is the great use of rhetoric? For from what has now been agreed on, of course, a man must most of all guard himself, so as not to do injustice, on the grounds that he will have evil enough. Isn't that so?

POL.: Certainly.

SOC.: And if either he himself or someone else of those he cares for does injustice, he will willingly go to that place where he will pay the just penalty as quickly as possible, to the judge as to the doctor, hurrying

480b lest the disease of injustice, become chronic, should make his soul fester with sores underneath and be incurable. Or what do we say, Polus, if our earlier agreements stand? Must not these things of necessity harmonize with those earlier ones in this way, but not in any other?

POL.: What indeed are we to say, Socrates?

SOC.: For speaking in defense of one's own injustice, therefore, or that of parents or comrades or children or fatherland when it does injustice, rhetoric will be of no use to us, Polus; except if someone takes it

480c to be of use for the opposite purpose, supposing that he must most of all accuse himself, and then whoever else of his relatives and friends happens at any time to do injustice, and not hide the unjust deed but bring it into the open, so as to pay the just penalty and become healthy, and compel both himself and others not to play the coward but to grit his teeth[59] and submit well and courageously as if

---

the Peloponnesian War. Thucydides at 4.78.3 contrasts dynasty with the rule of equal law (*isonomia*).

59. The Greek idiom literally is "to shut his eyes."

to a doctor for cutting and burning—pursuing what's good and fine, not taking account of what's painful, and if he has done unjust deeds

480d worthy of blows, submitting to beating; if worthy of bonds, submitting to being bound; if worthy of a fine, paying it; if worthy of banishment, going into exile; and if worthy of death, dying;—himself being the first accuser both of himself and of others that are relatives, and using rhetoric for this purpose, so that, their unjust deeds having become manifest, they may be released from the greatest evil, injustice. Are we to speak thus or are we not, Polus?

480e POL.: To me, Socrates, they seem strange indeed; but perhaps you make them agree with the things said before.

SOC.: So then, must either those earlier things too be undone, or must these of necessity follow?

POL.: Yes, that's the way this is.

SOC.: And turning on the other hand to the opposite, if indeed one must ever do evil to someone, either enemy or whomever—if only one does not oneself suffer injustice from the enemy, for of this one must beware—if the enemy does injustice to someone else, one must pro-

481a vide in every way, by acting and by speaking, that he not pay the just penalty nor go to the judge. And if he does go, one must contrive that the enemy get away and not pay the just penalty, but if he has stolen much gold, that he not give it back but keep it and spend it unjustly and godlessly on himself and his; and if he has done unjust deeds worthy of death, that he shall not die—above all that he never die but shall

481b be deathless in being wicked, and if not this, that he shall live for as long a time as possible in being such. For such things, Polus, rhetoric seems to me to be useful, since for him who isn't going to do injustice, there doesn't seem to me to be any great use for it, if indeed there even is some use, which nowhere in the earlier discussion came to light.

CAL.: Tell me, Chaerephon, is Socrates serious about these things or is he joking?[60]

CHAE.: To me, Callicles, he seems to be extraordinarily serious; but there's nothing like asking the man himself.[61]

---

60. Several important words are related to the root *pais*, child. *Paizein* means joking, sporting, or playing. *Paidia* is play. *Paideia* is education. *Ta paidika* is a boy or young man with whom an older man has an erotic relationship; though the usual translation is "favorite," I have translated "boyfriend," but it should be noted that the Greek conveys no implication of a reciprocal relationship.

61. Chaerephon's echo of Callicles' own language at 447c suggests that the dialogue is to begin anew here.

CAL.: By the gods, I certainly desire to do so! Tell me, Socrates, are we
481c   to take it that you are now being serious or joking? For if you are serious and these things you are saying happen to be true, wouldn't the
life of us human beings have been turned upside down and don't we
do, as it would appear, all the opposite things to what we ought?

SOC.: Callicles, if human beings did not have some feeling[62] that was
the same—some having one and others another—but if some one of
us suffered some private feeling different from what the others feel,
481d   it would not be too easy to point out one's own affection to the other.
I say this bearing in mind that you and I now happen to have suffered something that is the same: we are two lovers,[63] each in love
with two things—I with Alcibiades the son of Cleinias[64] and with
philosophy, and you with two things, the Athenian people and the
son of Pyrilampes.[65] And so I perceive you on each occasion unable,
terribly clever though you are, to contradict what your boyfriends
481e   say and how they say things are, but you turn yourself around up
and down. In the assembly, if, as you are saying something, the Athenian people denies that it is so, you turn around and say what it
wishes; and also in regard to this beautiful youth, the son of Pyrilampes, you have suffered other things of this sort. For you are not
able to oppose either the proposals or the speeches of your boyfriends; so that if, when on each occasion you say the things you say
on account of them, someone was amazed at how strange they are,

---

62. *Pathos,* the same word rendered "passive condition" at 476c, could also be translated
here "experience," but except as noted I have reserved that term for *empeiria* (as at 448c).
"Affection" translates *pathēma.* I often translate the related verb "suffer."

63. The word here is a participle cognate with *erōs;* see note on *erōs* and *phil-* at 513c.

64. Alcibiades was wealthy, of a prominent family (he was the nephew of Pericles), beautiful, gifted, and ambitious. He supported the Sicilian expedition, through which Athens re-
sumed the Peloponnesian War in 415, thus putting an end to the Peace of Nicias, and was
named one of the three generals. Recalled to face charges of mutilating sacred statues of
Hermes erected at various places throughout Athens and of violating the sanctity of the
Eleusinian Mysteries, and fearing death from his political opponents, he went over to the
Spartan side. Later he negotiated with Persia, Sparta, and Athens, and eventually was recalled by Athens to a position of leadership. He is the central character in the second half of
Thucydides' *History.* Two Platonic dialogues carry his name as title. Plato recounts Alci-
biades' drunken, frank, eloquent speech about his relation to Socrates in the *Symposium*
(212d–223a).

65. The Athenian *dēmos* and *Dēmos* the son of Pyrilampes, who was famous for his beauty
and also for lack of intelligence (Aristophanes, *Wasps* 98 and fragment of Eupolis's *Poleis*
[213 Kock]). "People" translates *dēmos,* but it should be noted that, whereas "people" has
an all-inclusive connotation, Greek *dēmos* tends to emphasize the lower classes as distinguished from the nobility, wealthy, or great.

you might perhaps say to him, if you wished to speak the truth, that
482a unless someone will make your boyfriends desist from these speeches,
you will never stop saying these things either. Consider accordingly
that you must hear other things of this sort from me too, and do not
be amazed that I say them, but stop my boyfriend, philosophy, from
saying them. For, my friend and comrade, philosophy always says
what you now hear from me and is much less capricious with me
than the other boyfriend: for this fellow of Cleinias's family presents
various speeches at various times, whereas philosophy always pre-
482b sents the same and says what you are now amazed at—and you were
present yourself to hear the things said. So then either refute that one,
as I was saying just a while ago, by showing that doing injustice and
not paying the just penalty when one does injustice are not the utmost of all evils; or else, if you leave this unrefuted—by the dog, the
god of the Egyptians!—Callicles will not agree with you, Callicles,
but will be dissonant in his whole life. And yet I think, you best of
men, it is superior[66] that my lyre be out of tune and dissonant, and
the chorus I might provide for the public, and that most human be-
482c ings disagree with me and say contradictory things, rather than that
I, being one man, should be discordant with myself and say contradictory things.

CAL.: Socrates, you seem to me to act like a youth in the arguments,[67]
like the popular speaker you truly are; and now you make this popular speech since Polus has suffered the same experience[68] that he accuses Gorgias of suffering in regard to you. For doubtless he said that
when Gorgias was asked by you whether, when someone who wished
482d to learn rhetoric but who did not know the just things came to him,
Gorgias would teach him, Gorgias felt ashamed and said he would
teach, on account of the custom of human beings, in that they would
be angry if someone said no. Now, through this agreement he was
compelled to say things that contradicted himself; and this is the
very thing you are fond of. And at that time he laughed at you, correctly, at least as it seems to me; but now in turn he has suffered this

66. *Kreittōn* means stronger, superior, better. I have usually used "stronger," but sometimes "superior." The famous old accusation against Socrates of "making the weaker argument stronger" (*Apology* 19b) uses this same word, whose range of meanings plays a key
role in Socrates' upcoming refutation of Callicles.
67. That is, to display the excess or extravagance of youth; compare Socrates' use of the
same charge against Lysias (*Phaedrus* 235a).
68. *Pathos*: see note at 481c.

same thing. And I for one do not admire Polus on this very point, that
he conceded to you that doing injustice is more shameful than suf-
482e fering injustice; for from this agreement he himself in turn got his feet
entangled and his mouth gagged by you in the speeches, since he felt
ashamed to say what he thought. For, Socrates, you really lead the
discussion into such tiresome things, suited to a popular speaker—
while claiming to pursue the truth—things that are not fine by nature, but by convention. And in most cases these things are opposed
to each other, nature and convention;[69] if, therefore, someone feels
483a ashamed and doesn't dare say what he thinks, he is compelled to say
contradictory things. And now, having thoroughly understood this
piece of wisdom, you work evil in the arguments: if someone speaks
of things according to convention, you slip in questions about things
according to nature, and if he speaks of the things of nature, you ask
about the things of convention. Just as, for an immediate example, in
these matters of doing injustice and suffering injustice, when Polus
spoke of the more shameful according to convention, you pursued
the argument according to nature.[70] For by nature, everything is more
shameful that is also worse, such as[71] suffering injustice, whereas
by convention doing injustice is more shameful. Nor does this mis-
483b fortune, suffering injustice, belong to a man,[72] but to some slave for
whom it is superior to die than to live, who, suffering injustice and
being trampled in the mud, is unable to help himself or anyone else
he cares for. But, I think, those who set down the laws are the weak
human beings and the many. It is therefore in reference to themselves
and their own advantage that they set down laws and praise their
483c praises and blame their blames: frightening away the more forceful
human beings and those with power to have more, so that they won't
have more than themselves, they say that taking more is shameful

69. *Nomos*, translated "law" or "convention," includes written law, unwritten law, custom, and prevalent opinion. The root idea involves distribution, allotment (verb *nemein*). Pre-Socratic philosophy discovered and elaborated the difference between convention and nature, *phusis*, whose related verb means "to grow." Things that exist by nature, such as fire, are the same here and in Persia, whereas things that exist by convention, such as burial practices, differ (see Aristotle, *Nicomachean Ethics* 5.1134b).
70. The manuscripts read *nomon* instead of *logon* ("argument"), which would yield the puzzling meaning "you pursued convention according to nature."
71. Some editors, including Dodds, add this "such as." Without it, the apposition of "suffering injustice" with "everything" is not quite logical (which, if the correct text, might reflect the passionate character of Callicles' speech).
72. The term is the emphatically male *anēr* (see note at 447c).

and unjust, and that doing injustice is this—seeking to have more than the others. For they are quite contented, I think, if they themselves have an equal share, since they are lowlier.

Now it's on account of these things that this, seeking to have more than the many, is said by convention to be unjust and shameful, and they call it doing injustice. But nature herself, I think, reveals that this 483d very thing is just, for the better to have more than the worse and the more powerful than the less powerful. And it is clear in many places that these things are so: both among the other animals and in whole cities and races[73] of human beings, the just has been decided thus, for the stronger to rule the weaker and to have more. Indeed, making use of what kind of justice did Xerxes lead his army against Greece, 483e or his father against the Scythians?[74] Or one could tell of myriad other such cases. Indeed I think these men do these things according to the nature of the just, and yes, by Zeus, according to the law of nature[75]—though perhaps not according to this one that we set down. By molding the best and most forceful of us, catching them young, like lions, subduing them by charms and bewitching them, we re- 484a duce them to slavery, saying that one must have an equal share and that this is the noble and the just. But, I think, if a man having a sufficient nature comes into being, he shakes off and breaks through all these things and gets away, trampling underfoot our writings, spells, charms, and the laws that are all against nature, and the slave rises 484b up to be revealed as our master; and there the justice of nature shines forth. And Pindar too seems to me to point to what I'm saying in the ode in which he says that "Law, the king of all mortals and immortals"; and this indeed, he says, "leads, making what is most violent just, with highest hand; I judge so from the works of Heracles, since—without payment—. . ." he says something like this—for I do not know the ode—he says that he drove off the cows though he

73. *Genos:* family, posterity, tribe, clan, race, stock, kin; sometimes a subdivision of *ethnos* (nation, people), though here perhaps the same.
74. Xerxes' invasion of Greece (partly to avenge the defeat at Marathon of his father's earlier invasion) ended in naval defeat at Salamis and defeat on land at Plataea; in the aftermath of these Persian defeats, Athens began its move under the leadership of Themistocles toward imperial power. Darius's invasion of Scythia also ended in defeat. On Persian kings, see note at 470e. One could imagine a rather more moralistic interpretation of these same facts, contrary to Callicles' point.
75. This phrase "law of nature," first attested here in Greek literature, in view of the distinction between law (or convention) and nature, has a paradoxical character, of which Callicles' oath seems to show him to be somehow aware.

484c   didn't buy them nor did Geryon give them, on the grounds that this is the just by nature, that the worse and weaker men's cows and all other possessions belong to the better and stronger man.[76]

The truth, therefore, is thus, and you will know it if you proceed to greater things, once you have let philosophy drop. For philosophy, to be sure, Socrates, is a graceful thing, if someone engages in it in due measure at the proper age; but if he fritters his time away in it further than is needed, it is the corruption of human beings.[77] For even if he is of an altogether good nature and philosophizes far along in age, he must of necessity become inexperienced in all those things that one

484d   who is to be a noble and good man, and well reputed, must have experience of. And indeed they become inexperienced in the laws of the city, in the speeches one must use to associate with human beings in dealings both privately and publicly, in human pleasures and desires, and in sum they become all in all inexperienced in customs and characters. Whenever, therefore, they enter into some private or po-

484e   litical action, they become ridiculous; just as, I think, political men are ridiculous, whenever they in turn enter into your pastimes and speeches. For Euripides' saying comes to pass: each one is brilliant in this, and presses on to this, "allotting the greatest part of the day to

485a   this, where he happens to be at his best." And he flees from wherever he is undistinguished and reviles this, but praises the other thing out of goodwill toward himself, thinking that in this manner he praises himself. But I think the most correct thing is to partake of both. It is fine to partake of philosophy to the extent that it is for the sake of education, and it is not shameful to philosophize when one is a lad. But when a human being who is already rather older still philosophizes, the thing becomes ridiculous, Socrates, and I feel toward those who

485b   philosophize something very much like what I feel toward those who mumble and play around childishly. For whenever I see a small child, to whom it is still proper to talk in this manner, mumbling and playing around, I rejoice and it appears graceful to me, befitting a free man, and suitable to the small child's age; whereas when I hear a little boy talking distinctly, the thing seems to me to be rather disagreeable, vexes my ears, and seems to me to be something slavish.

---

76. Of this poem by the fifth-century Theban poet Pindar, only fragments are preserved; the same fragment is referred to in the *Laws* at 690b and quoted at 715a. See note at *Gorgias* 487c.
77. This corruption uses the same root word as the corrupting that Socrates will later be accused of inflicting on Athens's youth.

485c   But whenever one hears a man mumbling or sees him playing around childishly, it appears ridiculous, unmanly, and deserving of a beating. So then, I feel this same thing toward those who philosophize, too. For seeing philosophy in a young lad, I admire it, and it seems to me fitting, and I consider this human being to be a free man, whereas the one who does not philosophize I consider illiberal, someone who
485d   will never deem himself worthy of any fine and noble[78] affair. But whenever I see an older man still philosophizing and not released from it, this man, Socrates, surely seems to me to need a beating. For as I was saying just now, it falls to this man, even if he is of an altogether good nature, to become unmanly through fleeing the central area of the city and the agoras, in which the poet says men "become highly distinguished,"[79] and through sinking down into living the
485e   rest of his life whispering with three or four lads in a corner, never to give voice to anything free or great or sufficient.

But I, Socrates, am fairly friendly toward you; so I have now probably felt what Euripides' Zethus felt toward Amphion, of which I made mention.[80] And indeed some things come upon me to say to you such as that man said to his brother, that "You are careless, Socrates, of the things that you ought to take care of, and having received by fate so noble a soul's nature, you make yourself conspicu-
486a   ous in a shape belonging to a lad; and you would not contribute a speech correctly to the councils of justice, nor cry out something probable or persuasive, nor advise any new proposal on another's behalf." And yet, Socrates my friend—and do not be annoyed at me, for I shall speak with goodwill toward you—does it not seem to you to be a shameful thing to be in such a condition as I think you and the others are, who are forever pushing further on in philosophy? For now, if someone seized you or anybody else of that sort of people and carried you off to prison, claiming that you were doing an injustice when you were not, you know that you would not have anything of
486b   use to do for yourself, but you would be dizzy and gaping, without anything to say; and when you stood up in the law court, happening

78. "Noble" here and in 485e is *gennaios*, which I've usually translated "nobly born" (with "noble" usually reserved for *kalos*).
79. The poet, of course, is Homer: *Iliad* 9.441. "Agora" refers both to marketplaces and to places of public assembly, with the latter dominant here. See the mention of the agora at 447a.
80. Euripides' lost play *Antiope* presented a debate between the active life represented by the shepherd Zethus and the artistic or contemplative life represented by his brother, Amphion.

to face a very lowly and vicious accuser, you would die, if he wished
to demand the death penalty for you. Yet "how can this be a wise
thing," Socrates, "an art that took a man[81] with a good nature and
made him worse," unable to help himself or to save either himself or
486c   anyone else from the greatest dangers, but liable to be stripped of his
whole substance by his enemies and to live absolutely unhonored[82]
in the city? To say something rather rude—it is possible to strike such
a man a crack on the jaw without paying the just penalty. Rather,
good man, be persuaded by me, stop refuting, "practice the good
music" of affairs, and practice there whence "you will be reputed to
think intelligently, giving up to others these refined subtleties"—
whether one must say they are silliness or drivel—"from which you
will dwell in an empty house," envying not the men who make refu-
486d   tations over these small matters, but those who have livelihood, reputation, and many other good things.[83]

soc.: If I happened to have a golden soul, Callicles, would you not
think I'd be pleased to find one of those stones with which they test
gold—the best such stone, so that when I had applied the soul to it,
if that stone agreed with me that the soul had been finely taken care
of, I would at last be on the point of knowing well that I am in sufficiently good condition and have no further need for another touchstone?

486e   cal.: In regard to what now do you ask this, Socrates?

soc.: I shall tell you now. I think that, having fallen in with you, I
have fallen in with a godsend of that sort.

cal.: How so?

soc.: Know well that, if you agree with me on the things that my soul
holds opinions about, these at last are the true things themselves. For
487a   I am reflecting that he who is going to make a sufficient test of a
soul's living correctly or not must in fact have three things, all of
which you have: knowledge, goodwill, and outspokenness. For I fall
in with many who are not able to test me on account of not being

81. The poetic word *phōs*, which is often contrasted as mortal with immortal gods, suggests
another quotation from *Antiope*.

82. The word carries also the meaning of being deprived of legal rights in the city, in
which case one could be subject to summary arrest and jailing (as Callicles has just suggested at 486a).

83. This critique of Socrates' manner of investigating and refuting reminds of the very similar criticism stated by the Sophist Hippias near the end of the *Hippias Major* (304a–b), in
which Socrates and Hippias seek to state what the beautiful (noble, fine) is.

wise as you are; and others are wise but are not willing to tell me the truth on account of not caring for me as you do; and these two for-

487b eigners here, Gorgias and Polus, are wise and friends of mine, but rather too lacking in outspokenness and too sensitive to shame, more so than is needful. And how could they not be? Since indeed they have advanced so far into the sense of shame that—on account of feeling shame—each one of them dares to contradict himself in front of many human beings, and this concerning the greatest things. But you have all those things that the others do not have; for you have been sufficiently educated, as many of the Athenians would say, and

487c you are of goodwill toward me. What evidence do I use? I shall tell you. I know, Callicles, that four of you have become partners in wisdom: you, Teisandros of Aphidnae, Andron son of Androtion, and Nausicydes of Cholarges.[84] And once I overheard you taking counsel on how far one must practice wisdom, and I know that some opinion of the following sort prevailed among you: you urged each other not

487d to be eager to philosophize to the point of precision, but to be cautious lest, by becoming wiser beyond what is needful, you should be corrupted unawares. Since, therefore, I hear you giving the same counsels to me as to your own closest comrades, it is sufficient evidence for me that you are truly of goodwill toward me. And that you are indeed able to be outspoken and not to feel shame, you yourself assert, and the speech that you were making a little while ago agrees with

487e you. So this is how it stands now about these things: when you agree with me on something in the speeches, this will at last have been sufficiently tested by you and me, and there will be no further need to carry it back to another touchstone. For you would never have conceded it either through a lack of wisdom or through an excess of sense of shame, nor again would you concede it to deceive me; for you are a friend to me, as you yourself say. Your and my agreement, therefore, will really at last attain the goal of truth. And the investigation about the things for which you censured me, Callicles, is the finest of all: what sort of man one ought to be and what one ought to pursue

84. Nothing certain is known of the first and third mentioned; they are probably wealthy young men. Andron son of Androtion was one of the oligarchic Four Hundred (see note at 472b). He is present at the gathering of Sophists at Callias's house depicted in the *Protagoras*, among those surrounding the Sophist Hippias (315c). At a crucial juncture of the conversation Hippias states a view like Pindar's as quoted by Callicles: "I consider you all kin and relatives and citizens by nature, not by law; for by nature like is kin to like, but law, being the tyrant of human beings, violently forces many things against nature" (337c–d).

488a and how far, for both an older and a younger man. For if I am doing something incorrectly in the course of my life, know well that I do not make this error voluntarily but through my lack of learning. So then, just as you began to admonish me, do not give up but point out to me sufficiently what this is that I must pursue and in what way I might acquire it. And if you catch me agreeing with you now but at a later time not doing those things that I have agreed on, consider me
488b a complete dolt and never admonish me any more later on, on the grounds that I'm worth nothing.

Now take it up again for me from the beginning. How do both you and Pindar say the just stands—the just according to nature, that is? That the stronger carry off by violence the weaker men's things, that the superior rule the worse men, and that the better have more than the lowlier?[85] You're not saying that the just is anything else, or do I remember correctly?

CAL.: Indeed I said these things then and I say them now.

SOC.: And do you call the same man superior and stronger? For at
488c that time I was surely not able to understand from you what on earth you mean. Are you calling the mightier men stronger, and the feebler men ought to obey the mightier man, as in my opinion you were pointing out at that time, saying how big cities advance against small ones in accordance with the just by nature, because they are stronger and mightier, on the grounds that the stronger and mightier and superior are the same thing? Or is it possible for one to be superior but weaker and feebler, and to be stronger but more vicious? Or is the
488d boundary of the superior and the stronger the same? Define this very thing distinctly for me: are the stronger and the superior and the mightier the same or different?[86]

CAL.: Well, I say to you distinctly that they are the same.

SOC.: So then, are the many stronger than the one according to nature? They surely do set down laws upon the one, as you too were saying just now.

CAL.: How could they not be?

SOC.: The lawful usages of the many, therefore, are those of the stronger.

---

85. *Beltiōn* ("superior") and *ameinōn* ("better") are synonomous, though perhaps the former has a stronger connotation of social or moral superiority.

86. Socrates makes similar use of the broad range of meaning of *kreittōn* ("stronger," see note at 482b) in the first step of his refutation of Thrasymachus's assertion that justice is the advantage of the stronger (*Republic* 338c–d).

CAL.: Certainly.

488e   SOC.: So then, are they those of the superior? For the stronger are, I suppose, superior, according to your argument.[87]

cal.: Yes.

SOC.: So then are the lawful usages of these people fine according to nature, since they are stronger?

CAL.: I say so.

SOC.: Well then don't the many customarily hold, as again you were saying just now, that having an equal share is just and that doing in-
489a   justice is more shameful than suffering injustice? Are these things so or not? And don't you in turn get caught here feeling shame. Do the many customarily hold, or not, that having an equal share but not having more is just, and that doing injustice is more shameful than suffering injustice? Do not begrudge answering me this, Callicles, so that, if you agree with me, I may at last receive confirmation from you, seeing that a man sufficient at discerning things has agreed.

CAL.: Well, the many, at any rate, customarily hold this view.

SOC.: It is not only by convention, therefore, that doing injustice is
489b   more shameful than suffering injustice, and that having an equal share is just; but also by nature. So probably you were not saying true things earlier and you did not accuse me correctly when you said that convention and nature are opposed, and that I too have observed this and then work evil in the arguments, by leading someone toward convention if he speaks according to nature, and toward nature if he speaks according to convention.

CAL.: This man here will not stop driveling! Tell me, Socrates, are you not ashamed at your age to hunt after words and, if someone errs in
489c   his utterance, to take this as a godsend? Do you think I mean that being stronger men is anything other than being superior men? Haven't I long been saying to you that I assert the superior and the stronger to be the same? Or do you think I am saying that, if a rabble of slaves and human beings of all sorts, worth nothing except perhaps for the exertion of bodily might, was collected together, and if these people asserted some things, these things are lawful?

SOC.: So be it, most wise Callicles. Is this what you're saying?

CAL.: Yes indeed.

---

87. The manuscripts read *polu* rather than *pou*; this would then read "the stronger are much superior, according to your argument."

489d SOC.: Well, you demonic man,[88] I myself have also long been guessing that by the stronger you mean some such thing, and I've been
asking in eager longing to know distinctly what you mean. For doubtless you, at any rate, do not consider two as superior to one, nor your
slaves as superior to you, because they are mightier than you. But tell
us again from the beginning, what on earth do you mean by the superior men, since you don't mean the mightier? And, you amazing
man, instruct me more gently, so that I won't stop attending your
school.

489e CAL.: You are being ironical, Socrates.[89]

SOC.: By Zethus, whom you made use of just now to say many ironical things toward me! But come, tell us: who do you say are the superior men?

CAL.: The better men, I say.

SOC.: Now then do you see that you yourself are saying words but
making nothing clear? Won't you say whether by the superior and
stronger men you mean the more intelligent[90] or certain others?

CAL.: Yes indeed, by Zeus, I do mean these, and emphatically so!

490a SOC.: Many times, therefore, one man who thinks intelligently is
stronger according to your argument than ten thousand who do not,
and this man ought to rule, and those be ruled, and the ruler have
more than the ruled; for this in my opinion is what you wish to say—
and I am not hunting after little phrases[91]—if the one is stronger than
the ten thousand.

CAL.: This is indeed what I mean. For I think that the just by nature is
this, for one who is superior and more intelligent both to rule and to
have more than the lowlier ones.

88. A *daimōn* is some kind of superhuman being; one might translate *daimonios* "divine,"
but in the *Symposium* Socrates presents the view that *daimones* (such as *Erōs*, [erotic] love)
are beings in between, and mediating between, gods and human beings. Earlier in this dialogue (456a), he suggested that the power of rhetoric might be demonic. The most frequent
word for happy, *eudaimōn*, would mean having a good *daimōn*.
89. The complex notion of irony may involve speaking with twofold meaning and speaking so as to hide a claim to superiority; in the present context it doubtless contrasts with the
outspokenness discussed by Socrates at 487b.
90. *Phronimos,* a rather new word first found in Sophocles' *Ajax,* was later used by Aristotle
for the prudent man or the man of practical wisdom. Callicles used the related verb *phronein*
at 486c in urging Socrates to seek the reputation of "thinking intelligently" (or prudently or
sensibly). *Sōphrōn* (which I usually translate "moderate" but must sometimes render "of
sound mind," as opposed to mad) shares the same root *phrēn* (heart, mind, wits).
91. Accepting Badham's conjecture *rhēmatia* (reported by Dodds); the manuscript text
might yield the sense, "not hunting [you] with a phrase."

490b   soc.: Stop right there. What on earth are you saying now in turn? If we are many crowded together in the same place, just as now, and we have much food and drink in common, and we are of all sorts, some mighty, some feeble, and one of us, being a doctor, is more intelligent about these things, and—as is likely—he is mightier than some, feebler than others—then will not this man, being more intelligent than we, be superior and stronger in regard to these things?

CAL.: Certainly.

490c   soc.: Should he then have more of this food than we, because he is superior? Or ought that man through his ruling to distribute it all, and he should not take more by consuming it all and using it up for his own body—if he is not to pay a fine[92]—but should have more than some and less than others? And if he happens to be feeblest of all, should the most superior man have the least of all, Callicles? Isn't this how it is, good man?

CAL.: You are talking of food and drink and doctors and drivel; but 490d   this is not what I mean.

soc.: Aren't you saying that the more intelligent man is superior? Say yes or no.

CAL.: I am.

soc.: Well, ought not the superior man to have more?

CAL.: Not of food, though, nor of drink.

soc.: I understand, but perhaps of clothing; and the man most skilled in weaving ought to have the biggest cloak and go around clothed in the most numerous and most beautiful ones?

CAL.: What's this about cloaks?[93]

soc.: Well, in regard to shoes, clearly the most intelligent and most 490e   superior man in these things ought to take more. Perhaps the cobbler ought to have the biggest shoes and walk around shod with the most numerous ones.

CAL.: What's this about shoes? You keep on driveling.

soc.: But if you don't mean things of this sort, perhaps things of the following sort: a man skilled in farming, for example, intelligent about land, and fine and good—this man now ought perhaps to take more seeds and use as much seed as possible for his own land.

CAL.: How you always say the same things, Socrates!

92. Or suffer loss—that is, one supposes, in health.
93. Literally, "What sort of cloaks?" This form of riposte, frequent in comedy, has also the force of an exclamation of disbelief—perhaps "Cloaks, my foot!"

soc.: Not only that, Callicles, but also about the same things.[94]

491a cal.: By the gods, you simply[95] always talk without stopping about cobbliers, clothiers, cooks, and doctors, as if our speech were about these people!

soc.: So won't you then say whom it is about? In having more of what things does the stronger and more intelligent man justly take more? Or will you neither suffer me to suggest nor speak for yourself?

cal.: But I have been saying it for a long time now. First, then, by those who are stronger I mean neither cobblers nor cooks, but those

491b who are intelligent in regard to the affairs of the city and in what way they may be well governed—and not only intelligent but also courageous, being sufficient to accomplish what they intend and not flinching through softness of soul.

soc.: Do you see, most superior Callicles, how you do not accuse me of the same things as I do you? For you assert that I always say the same things and find fault with me; but I assert the opposite of you, that you never say the same things about the same things, but at that

491c time you were defining the superior and stronger as the mightier, and again as the more intelligent, and now in turn you arrive with something else: certain more courageous men are said by you to be the stronger and superior. Well, good man, speak and have done:[96] who on earth do you say are the superior and stronger, and in regard to what?

cal.: But indeed I have already said: those who are intelligent in regard to the affairs of the city and courageous. For it is fitting that

491d these men rule the cities; and the just is this, that these, the rulers, have more than the others, the ruled.

soc.: But what in relation to themselves, comrade?

cal.: What in the world?

soc.: Rulers or ruled?

cal.: What do you mean?

soc.: I mean that each one himself rules himself. Or is there no need of this, that he rule himself, but only that he rule the others?

94. A strikingly similar exchange takes place between the Sophist Hippias and Socrates in Xenophon's *Memorabilia* (4.4.6). Whereas intellectuals (whether sophists or rhetoricians), like Hippias there, often pride themselves on the novelty of what they have to say, Socrates stresses (482a, 509a) that philosophy says ever the same things.

95. *Atechnōs* (simply, absolutely) has the root meaning "without art."

96. More literally, "be released [from it]."

CAL.: What do you mean, ruling himself?

SOC.: Nothing complicated[97] but just what the many mean: being
491e   moderate and in control of oneself, ruling the pleasures and desires
that are in oneself.

CAL.: What a pleasant fellow you are—you're saying that the moderate are the foolish!

SOC.: How so? There's nobody who would not understand that this
is not what I'm saying.

CAL.: Yes, it most certainly is, Socrates. Since how would a human
being become happy while being a slave to anyone at all? No, this is
the fine and just according to nature, which I am now telling you outspokenly: the man who will live correctly must let his own desires be
492a   as great as possible and not chasten them, and he must be sufficient
to serve them, when they are as great as possible, through courage
and intelligence, and to fill them up with the things for which desire
arises on each occasion. But this, I think, is not possible for the many;
wherefore they blame such men because of shame, hiding their own
incapacity, and they say that intemperance is surely a shameful thing
(as I was saying earlier), enslaving the human beings who are superior in their nature; unable themselves to supply satisfaction for their
492b   pleasures, they praise moderation and justice because of their own
unmanliness. Because, for those for whom it is possible from the beginning to be either sons of kings or themselves by nature sufficient
to supply for themselves some rule or tyranny or dynasty—what in
truth would be more shameful and worse than moderation and justice for these human beings, and that they, who can enjoy the good
things (and with no one blocking their path), should impose a master on themselves, the law and speech and blame of the many human
492c   beings? Or how would they not have become wretched under the
sway of this fine thing, justice and moderation, when they distribute
nothing more to their own friends than to enemies—and this while
ruling in their own city? But in truth, Socrates, which you claim to
pursue, this is how it is: luxury, intemperance, and freedom, when
they have support—this is virtue and happiness; and those other
things, the fine pretenses, the agreements of human beings against
nature, are drivel and worth nothing.

492d   SOC.: In no ignobly born manner, at any rate, Callicles, do you forge
ahead in speech, outspokenly. For you are now saying distinctly

---

97. Literally, "multicolored" (a term Socrates applies to democracy in the *Republic,* at 557c).

what the others think but are unwilling to say. I therefore beg of you in no way to slacken, so that how one must live may really become thoroughly clear. And tell me: do you assert that one must not chasten the desires, if one is to be such as one should, but let them be as great as possible and prepare satisfaction for them from any place whatsoever, and that this is virtue?

492e

CAL.: That is what I assert.

SOC.: Then those who need nothing are not correctly said to be happy?

CAL.: No, for in this way stones and corpses would be happiest.

SOC.: But surely the life of those you are talking about is also terrible. And indeed I would not be amazed if what Euripides says is true in these lines, where he says, "Who knows, if living is being dead, and

493a

being dead is living?"[98] And perhaps really we are dead; for I'm sure I have also heard from some one of the wise that we are now dead and our body is a tomb,[99] and this part[100] of the soul in which the desires exist happens to be such as to be persuaded and to change around up and down. And so a certain subtly refined myth-telling man, probably some Sicilian or Italian,[101] playing on its name, via *per-suadable* and *persuaded,* named it *jar,*[102] and named the thoughtless

493b

uninitiated;[103] and he said that this part of the uninitiated men's soul to which the desires belong, the intemperate and leaky part,[104] was a perforated jar—making the likeness on account of its insatiableness. This man surely points out what contradicts you, Callicles: that of those in Hades—meaning the unseen[105]—these, the uninitiated, are

98. The lines come from either the *Phrixus* or the *Polyidos,* both lost; Aristophanes mocks the lines in the *Frogs* (1082, 1477–78).

99. The Greek has a fine sound: *to sōma . . . sēma.*

100. "Part" is added, but "aspect" could be equally appropriate; the Greek is just *touto* ("this [thing]").

101. Dodds argues that one must take care to distinguish the myth's author, who probably composed an old religious poem (quite possibly Orphic) about the sufferings of the uninitiated in Hades, from the wise man (most likely a Pythagorean) who presented an allegorical interpretation of the myth to Socrates.

102. Wordplay abounds in this passage. Here *pithos* (jar) is linked to *pithanon* (persuadable) and *peistikon* or (Dodds's conjecture) *peiston* (persuaded).

103. Another pun: *anoētous amuētous.* The latter word, "uninitiated," comes from the verb *mueō* (to initiate); it may also remind of *muō* (to close, see note at 480c) and hence suggest "leaky" or "unstoppered."

104. I have followed Sauppe's emendation; Dodds's emendation would make this clause: "seeing its intemperate and leaky character."

105. Another etymology or pun: *Haidou* (genitive of *Haidēs*) and *aides* (from *a-idein,* not to see). This derivation of "Hades" is implied also at *Phaedo* 81c.

most wretched, and they carry water to their perforated jar with another such perforated thing, a sieve. And therefore he means—as the
493c   one who spoke to me said—that the sieve is the soul; he likens the soul of the thoughtless to a sieve since their soul is perforated, seeing that it cannot hold anything on account of disbelief and forgetfulness. Now probably these things are somewhat strange, but they make clear what I wish to point out to you—if I am somehow able—so as to persuade you to change your position, and instead of the insatiable and intemperate life to choose the orderly life, sufficient and
493d   satisfied with the things that are ever at hand. Well, am I persuading you somewhat and do you change to the position that the orderly are happier than the intemperate? Or even if I tell myths of many other such things, will you nonetheless not change anything?

CAL.: What you've just said is truer, Socrates.

SOC.: Come then, I'll tell you another likeness from the same school[106] as the one just now. Consider whether you are saying something of the following sort about the life of each, the moderate and the intemperate man: if each of two men had many jars, and those of the
493e   one were healthy and full (one of wine, one of honey, one of milk, and many others of many other things), and the sources of each of these things were scarce and difficult and to be supplied for oneself with many difficult toils; the one man, then, having filled his jars, conducts no more supplies to them nor gives any heed, but as regards these he is at rest; for the other man, just as for that one, the sources can be supplied but are difficult, the vessels are perforated and de-
494a   cayed, and he is always compelled, night and day, to fill them, or he suffers the utmost pains. Such being the life of each, are you really saying that the life of the intemperate man is happier than that of the orderly man? In saying these things, do I somewhat persuade you to grant that the orderly life is better than the intemperate, or do I not persuade you?

CAL.: You do not persuade me, Socrates. For that man who has filled his jars no longer has any pleasure; indeed this, as I was saying just now, is living just like a stone, when one has been filled up, no longer
494b   either rejoicing or feeling pain. But living pleasantly consists in this, in keeping as much as possible flowing in.

---

106. *Gumnasion,* a place for (naked) bodily exercise; conversation and instruction might also take place there.

soc.: So if much flows in, is it then necessary that what goes away also be much, and that there be some big holes for the outflowings?

cal.: Yes, certainly.

soc.: You in turn mean some life of a stone-curlew,[107] though not indeed of a corpse or a stone. Now tell me: do you mean something such as to be hungry and, being hungry, to eat?

cal.: I do.

494c   soc.: And to be thirsty and, being thirsty, to drink?

cal.: That's what I mean, and also that one who has all the other desires and can fulfill them, rejoices and lives happily.

soc.: Well done, best of men! Now continue just as you began, and do not hold back through shame. Nor, it would appear, must I hold back through shame. Now first say whether it is living happily for one who is tickled and itches to have an ungrudging amount of scratching and to continue scratching his life long?

494d   cal.: How strange you are, Socrates, and simply[108] a popular speaker!

soc.: Surely that's why, Callicles, I astounded Polus and Gorgias and made them feel ashamed; but don't you be astounded or feel ashamed, for you are courageous. But only answer.

cal.: Well then, I do assert that he who scratches, too, would live pleasantly.

soc.: So if pleasantly, then also happily?

cal.: Certainly.

494e   soc.: Is this the case if he should scratch only his head—or what more shall I ask you? See, Callicles, what you will answer if someone asks you in succession all the things that follow on these. And the culmination of such things as these, the life of catamites,[109] is this not terrible and shameful and wretched? Or will you dare to say that these men are happy, if they have an ungrudging amount of what they want?

cal.: Are you not ashamed, Socrates, to lead the arguments into such things?

soc.: What, is it I who lead them there, nobly born man? Or is it he who asserts without restraint, just like that, that those who rejoice—

---

107. Dodds notes that the *charadrios* is a bird of messy habits and uncertain identity; the scholiast writes that it excretes at the same time that it eats.

108. *Atechnōs:* see note at 491a.

109. A *kinaidos*, catamite, is the passive object of homosexual love and intercourse. *Kephalaion*, "culmination," puns on *kephalē*, "head."

495a   in whatever way they may rejoice—are happy, and who does not distinguish among the pleasures what sort are good and what sort bad?
But tell us further now, whether you assert that the pleasant and the
good are the same, or whether there is some one of the pleasant
things that is not good?

CAL.: In order that the speech should not contradict me, if I assert that
they are different, I assert that they are the same.

SOC.: You are corrupting the first speeches, Callicles, and you would no
longer be sufficiently examining with me the things that are, if you're
going to speak contrary to how things seem in your own opinion.

495b   CAL.: And you too, Socrates.

SOC.: Well then, I too am not doing what's correct, if indeed I do this,
nor are you. But, blessed man, observe that the good is not this, rejoicing in all ways; for these many shameful things, just now hinted
at, are manifest consequences, if this is the case, and many other
things too.

CAL.: As you think, at any rate, Socrates.

SOC.: Do you really, Callicles, contend mightily for these things?

CAL.: I do.

495c   SOC.: Shall we then put our hand to this argument as if you are serious?

CAL.: Certainly, very much so.

SOC.: Come then, since that's how it seems, determine for me the following things. Do you perhaps call something knowledge?

CAL.: I do.

SOC.: And weren't you just now saying that along with knowledge
there is a certain courage?

CAL.: That's what I was saying.

SOC.: So then, weren't you saying that these are two, on the grounds
that courage is something different from knowledge?

CAL.: Very much so.

SOC.: And what about this? Do you say pleasure and knowledge are
the same or different?

495d   CAL.: Different, I suppose, you wisest man.

SOC.: And you say courage is different from pleasure?

CAL.: How could it not be?

SOC.: Come now, let us remember these things: that Callicles the
Acharnian[110] asserted that pleasant and good are the same, and that

110. With the formality of some legal proclamation, Socrates states the deme (political subdivision of Athens) to which Callicles belongs; he responds in kind.

knowledge and courage are different both from each other and from the good.

CAL.: And does Socrates of Alopece not agree with us on these things, or does he agree?

495e SOC.: He does not agree; nor do I think that Callicles will either, when he himself looks on himself correctly. For tell me, don't you think that those who are doing well have suffered the opposite experience[111] than those who are doing badly?

CAL.: I do.

SOC.: So then if these things are opposed to each other, must one of necessity be in the same condition concerning them that one is in concerning health and sickness? For a human being is not, I suppose, healthy and sick at the same time, nor is he released at the same time from health and sickness.

CAL.: What do you mean?

SOC.: For example, consider it in regard to any part of the body you
496a wish, taking it by itself. May a human being be sick in his eyes, which has the name ophthalmia?

CAL.: To be sure.

SOC.: And he is not, I suppose, also healthy at the same time in respect to them, is he?

CAL.: In no way whatsoever.

SOC.: What about when he is released from ophthalmia? Is he then released from health of the eyes too and does he end up having been released from both at the same time?

CAL.: Not in the least.

496b SOC.: For I think that becomes something amazing and irrational, doesn't it?

CAL.: Very much so.

SOC.: Rather, I think, he gets and loses each in turn?

CAL.: I say so.

SOC.: And so in the same way as regards strength and weakness?

CAL.: Yes.

SOC.: And speed and slowness?

CAL.: Certainly.

SOC.: And as regards good things and happiness and their opposites, bad things and wretchedness—does he get each in turn and lose each in turn?

111. *Pathos:* see note at 481c.

CAL.: Quite so, doubtless.

496c   SOC.: Then if we find some things that a human being is released from and that he has at the same time, clearly these would not be the good and the bad. Do we agree on these things? And answer when you have considered it very well.

CAL.: I do agree, extraordinarily so.

SOC.: Come then—to the things agreed on earlier. You were speaking of being hungry: did you mean this is pleasant or painful? I mean being hungry, by itself.

CAL.: I say painful; but the hungry man's eating is pleasant.

496d   SOC.: I do too; I understand. But then being hungry itself is painful, or isn't it?

CAL.: I say so.

SOC.: And so then is being thirsty?

CAL.: Very much so.

SOC.: Shall I then ask still more, or do you agree that all need and desire are painful?

CAL.: I agree, so don't ask.

SOC.: So be it. Do you not then assert that the thirsty man's drinking is pleasant?

CAL.: I do.

SOC.: So then the "thirsty" in what you are saying is, I suppose, feeling pain?

496e   CAL.: Yes.

SOC.: And drinking is both fulfillment of need and pleasure?

CAL.: Yes.

SOC.: So then you are speaking of rejoicing during the drinking?

CAL.: Very much indeed.

SOC.: When one is thirsty, that is.

CAL.: I say so.

SOC.: Feeling pain?

CAL.: Yes.

SOC.: Do you then perceive the consequence, that you are saying that the man feeling pain rejoices at the same time, when you speak of the thirsty man's drinking? Or does this not come into being at the same time in relation to the same place—whether of soul or of body, as you wish? For, I think, it makes no difference. Are these things so, or not?

CAL.: They are.

soc.: But surely you do assert that it is impossible for the man who is
497a doing well to do badly at the same time.

cal.: I do assert it.

soc.: And you have agreed that it is possible for the man suffering
pain to rejoice.

cal.: So it appears.

soc.: To rejoice, therefore, is not to do well nor is to suffer pain to do
badly, so that the pleasant comes to be different from the good.

cal.: I don't know what sophisms you are making, Socrates.

soc.: You know, but you are being coy,[112] Callicles; advance still further into what's ahead.

cal.: Why do you keep on with such silly talk?

497b soc.: So that you may know how wise you are to admonish me. Does
not each of us stop being thirsty and being pleased by drinking at the
same time?

cal.: I don't know what you are saying.

gor.: Don't, Callicles; but answer for our sake too, so that the arguments may be brought to an end.

cal.: But Socrates is always like this, Gorgias. He asks small things,
of little worth, and refutes them.

gor.: But what difference does it make to you? It is not at all your
honor involved here,[113] Callicles. Submit to Socrates' refuting however he wishes.

497c cal.: Then ask these small and narrow things of yours, since that's
how it seems good to Gorgias.

soc.: You are a happy one, Callicles, to have been initiated in the
great things before the small;[114] I did not think it was righteous.[115]

---

112. The verb *akkizein* (to feign indifference or stupidity, to be coy) comes from *Akko,* a
proverbially stupid woman.

113. This meaning of this phrase is uncertain. It might mean, as Dodds and several others
think, "it is not for you to estimate their value"; but I find it rather unlikely that Callicles
would simply accept this latter statement from Gorgias without objection.

114. To be initiated into the greater Eleusinian Mysteries required that one had been pre-
viously initiated into the lesser (at Agrae). These mysteries had to do with tales about
Demeter, the goddess of grain, and her daughter, Kore, Plutus, the god of wealth and of
the underworld, and Persephone; with the sowing and harvest of grain; and with death,
rebirth, and the possibilities of human immortality. At *Symposium* 210a, Diotima (in Socrates' account of what he learned from her about *erōs,* love) mentions levels of initiation
into mysteries.

115. *Themiton,* from *themis:* what has been set down, established, made law, especially by
usage or custom; often connoting divine sanction no less than human.

Answer, then, where you left off, whether each of us does not stop being thirsty and pleased at the same time.

CAL.: I say so.

SOC.: So then does he cease from hungers and the other desires and from pleasures at the same time?

CAL.: That is so.

497d SOC.: So then does he cease from pains and pleasures at the same time?

CAL.: Yes.

SOC.: But surely he does not cease from good things and bad things at the same time, as you agreed; but do you not agree now?

CAL.: I do; so what then?

SOC.: This, that good things do not turn out to be the same as pleasant, my friend, nor bad things as painful. For he ceases from some at the same time, and from others not, since they are different. How then would pleasant things be the same as good or painful as bad?

Now if you wish, look at it in the following way too; for I think it
497e isn't agreed on by you in this way. Observe: do you not call good men good because of the presence of good things, just as you call them beautiful in whom beauty is present?

CAL.: I do.

SOC.: What about this? Do you call fools and cowards good men? That's not what you did recently, but rather you meant the courageous and intelligent; or don't you call these men good?

CAL.: Yes I do, certainly.

SOC.: What about this? Have you ever seen a thoughtless child rejoicing?

CAL.: I have.

SOC.: And have you never yet seen a thoughtless man rejoicing?

CAL.: I think I have; but what of it?

498a SOC.: Nothing; just answer.

CAL.: I have seen it.

SOC.: What about this: a man who has intelligence feeling pain and rejoicing?

CAL.: I say so.

SOC.: Which rejoice and feel pain more, the intelligent or the fools?

CAL.: I think there's not much difference.

SOC.: Well, even this is enough. And have you seen a cowardly man in war?

CAL.: How could I not have?

soc.: Well then, when the enemies went away, which seemed to you to rejoice more, the cowardly or the courageous men?

498b CAL.: To me, both seemed to rejoice; the former perhaps more,[116] or if not, about equally.

soc.: It makes no difference. But the cowards, then, rejoice too?

CAL.: Very much so.

soc.: And the fools, it would appear.

CAL.: Yes.

soc.: And as the enemies advanced, do only the cowards feel pain, or do the courageous ones too?

CAL.: Both.

soc.: Equally, then?

CAL.: The cowards perhaps feel more.

soc.: And do they not rejoice more when the enemies go away?

CAL.: Perhaps.

soc.: So then the foolish and the intelligent and the cowardly and the courageous men feel pain and rejoice about equally, as you assert,

498c and the cowardly more than the courageous?

CAL.: I say so.

soc.: But surely the intelligent and courageous men are good, and the cowardly and foolish are bad?

CAL.: Yes.

soc.: Therefore the good and the bad rejoice and feel pain about equally?

CAL.: I say so.

soc.: So are the good and the bad therefore about equally good and bad? Or are the bad still more good?

498d CAL.: But by Zeus, I do not know what you are saying!

soc.: Don't you know that you are asserting that the good are good because of the presence of good things, and the bad because of bad things? And that the good things are pleasures and the bad things pains?

CAL.: I do.

soc.: So then are the good things, pleasures, present for those who rejoice, if indeed they are rejoicing?

CAL.: Indeed, how could they not be?

---

116. The manuscripts give "To me, both rather; or if not, about equally." I have translated Dodds's plausible addition to restore what seems to have dropped out.

soc.: So then with good things present, are those who rejoice good?

CAL.: Yes.

soc.: What about this? Are not the bad things, pains, present for those who suffer pain?

CAL.: They are present.

498e   soc.: And do you assert that the bad are bad because of the presence of bad things? Or do you no longer assert it?

CAL.: I do.

soc.: Are they who rejoice therefore good, and they who suffer pain bad?

CAL.: Certainly.

soc.: Those who do so more, more; and less, less; and about equally, about equally?

CAL.: Yes.

soc.: So are you then asserting that the intelligent and the fools and the cowards and the courageous rejoice and feel pain about equally, or even the cowards still more?

CAL.: I am.

soc.: Now sum up in common with me what follows for us from the things agreed on; for they say that it is fine to speak of and to exam-

499a   ine the fine things even two or three times. We assert that the intelligent and courageous man is good, don't we?

CAL.: Yes.

soc.: And that the fool and coward is bad?

CAL.: Certainly.

soc.: And in turn that the man who rejoices is good?

CAL.: Yes.

soc.: And that the man who suffers pain is bad?

CAL.: Necessarily.

soc.: And that the good man and the bad man suffer pain and rejoice equally, and perhaps the bad man even more?

CAL.: Yes.

soc.: So does the bad man then become good and bad equally with

499b   the good man, or even more good? Don't these things follow, as well as those earlier ones, if someone asserts that pleasant and good things are the same? Aren't these things necessarily so, Callicles?

CAL.: I have been listening to you for a long time now, Socrates, and agreeing right along, pondering that, if someone is joking and grants you anything, you are pleased with it and hold on to it just as young lads do. As if you thought that I or any other human being did not consider some pleasures better and others worse!

soc.: Oh! Oh! Callicles, how all-cunning[117] you are and how you treat
499c me like a child—at one time claiming that things are this way, and at another time that the same things are otherwise, deceiving me! And yet I did not think at the beginning that I was to be deceived by you voluntarily, since you were my friend. But now I have been played false, and it looks like it's necessary for me—according to the old saying—to make do with what is present and to accept from you this that is given. What you are now saying, as it would appear, is that there are some pleasures that are good, and some that are bad. Isn't that it?

499d cal.: Yes.

soc.: So are the beneficial ones therefore good, and the harmful ones bad?

cal.: Certainly.

soc.: And those that produce something good are beneficial, and those that produce something bad are bad?

cal.: I say so.

soc.: Do you then mean such pleasures as we were just now speaking of in regard to the body, in eating and drinking—now of these, are those good that produce health in the body, or strength or some
499e other virtue of the body, while those that produce the opposites of these things are bad?

cal.: Certainly.

soc.: So then is it the same way with pains too? Are some useful and some base?

cal.: How could they not be?

soc.: So must one then choose and practice the useful pleasures and pains?

cal.: Certainly.

soc.: But not the base ones?

cal.: Clearly.

soc.: For if you remember, it seemed to us—to Polus and me—that one must do all things for the sake of good things. Is this the way it seems to you too, that the end of all actions is the good, and that all

117. *Panourgos*, literally, a doer of everything, viz., someone who will stop at nothing, even a daring criminal.

500a   other things must be done for the sake of it but not it for the sake of
        the other things? Do you too vote with us, making a third?

        CAL.: I do.

        SOC.: One must therefore do both other things and pleasant things for
        the sake of good things, but not good ones for the sake of pleasant.

        CAL.: Certainly.

        SOC.: Does it then belong to every man to pick out from the pleasant
        things what sort are good and what sort bad, or is an artful[118] man
        needed for each thing?

        CAL.: An artful man.

        SOC.: Let us then recollect the things that I happened, again, to be say-
        ing to Polus and Gorgias. For I was saying, if you remember, that
500b   some contrivances exist that go as far as pleasure, prepare this very
        thing alone, and ignore the better and the worse; and some that come
        to know what is good and what is bad. And among those concerned
        with pleasures I put the experience (not art) of cookery, and among
        those concerned with the good, the medical art. And by the god of
        Friendship,[119] Callicles, do not yourself think that you ought to joke
        with me, nor answer whatever you happen upon contrary to how
500c   things seem to you, nor in turn take things from me as if I were jok-
        ing. For you see that our speeches are about this—and what would a
        human being who had even a little intelligence be more serious about
        than this? That is, in what way one must live, whether the life to
        which you urge me on, doing these things of a man, speaking among
        the people and practicing rhetoric and acting in politics in this way
        in which you now act in politics; or this life in philosophy; and in
        what respect it can be that this life differs from that one. Perhaps then
500d   it is best, as I attempted a while back, to distinguish, and having dis-
        tinguished and agreed with each other, if these lives are indeed two
        and distinct, to examine in what they differ from each other and
        which of them one ought to live. Now perhaps you do not yet un-
        derstand what I am saying.

        CAL.: Indeed not.

        SOC.: Well, I shall speak to you more clearly. Since you and I have
        agreed that some good exists and some pleasant exists, and the pleas-

118. A more natural translation today would be "an expert," but I have kept "artful" to
make clear the connection with the issue of what is and what is not an art (see note at 447c).
119. *Pros Philiou*, "by [?] of Friendship," is probably short for "by Zeus the god of Friendship" (an oath used at *Phaedrus* 234e).

ant is different from the good, and there is a certain caring for each of them and a contrivance for their possession, the pursuit of the pleas-
500e   ant and the pursuit of the good—but first either assent or not to this very thing. Do you assent?

CAL.: I say so.

SOC.: Come then, agree with me on what I was saying to these men too, if what I was saying seemed true to you then. I was saying, I suppose, that cookery does not seem to me to be an art, but experience;
501a   whereas medicine, I said, examines the nature of him of whom it takes care and the cause of the things that it does, and it has a reasoned account to give of each of these things, medicine does. But the other—its care is wholly with pleasure, and it proceeds altogether artlessly toward pleasure, without having examined to any degree the nature of pleasure or the cause, all in all irrationally,[120] making virtually no distinct enumeration, but by routine and experience sav-
501b   ing only the memory of what usually comes about, by which then it also provides pleasures. First consider, therefore, whether these things seem to you to be stated in a sufficient manner, and whether certain other such occupations concerned with the soul too seem to exist, some of which are artful, having a certain forethought for the best as regards the soul, and some of which make light of this, but have examined—in this case as in the former—only the soul's pleasure, and in what way it may come into being for the soul, whether it is a better or a worse one of the pleasures, neither examining nor caring
501c   about anything but gratification alone, whether better or worse. For to me, Callicles, they do seem to exist, and I for one assert that this sort of thing is flattery, concerned with body and soul and anything else of whose pleasure someone takes care while having no consideration of better and worse. Now do you set down the same opinion with us about these things or do you speak against it?

CAL.: Not I; but I grant it, so that your argument may be brought to an end and I may gratify Gorgias here.
501d   SOC.: And is this the case concerning one soul, but not two or many?

CAL.: No, but also concerning two or many.

SOC.: Is it then possible to gratify them in crowds at the same time, without any consideration of the best?

---

120. *Alogōs*, "irrationally" or without a reasoned account; paralleling *atechnōs*, "artlessly" or without art.

CAL.: I think so.

SOC.: Are you then able to say what the pursuits are that do this? Or rather if you wish, as I ask, say yes when it seems to you to be one of 501e these, and say no when it doesn't. First let us consider flute playing.[121] Doesn't it seem to you to be such a one, Callicles—to pursue only our pleasure and to give heed to nothing else?

CAL.: It seems so to me.

SOC.: Is it then likewise with all of this sort, such as cithara playing in competitions?

CAL.: Yes.

SOC.: And how about the training of choruses and the composition of dithyrambs?[122] Don't you find it plainly of this sort? Or do you think that Cinesias the son of Meles paid any heed to how he would say something such that the hearers would become better from it, rather 502a than how he was to gratify the mob of spectators?

CAL.: It's clearly this, Socrates, at least as regards Cinesias.

SOC.: What about his father, Meles? Did he in your opinion sing to the cithara with a view to the best? Or did that man not even sing with a view to the most pleasant? For his singing used to pain the spectators. But consider now whether all singing to the cithara and composing of dithyrambs have not in your opinion been discovered for the sake of pleasure.

CAL.: It seems so to me.

502b SOC.: And the august[123] and amazing one itself, the composing of tragedy—toward what is it serious? As it seems to you, is its attempt and seriousness only to gratify the spectators, or also if something is pleasant and gratifying to them but base, to fight not to say this, and if something happens to be unpleasant and beneficial, to fight to say and sing this, whether they rejoice or not? In which way in your opinion has the composing of tragedies been prepared?

---

121. I use the traditional translation, "flute," of *aulos*, which in fact was an ancient reed instrument rather more like an oboe or clarinet. Dodds notes that the instrument was used for musical accompaniment in the theater but was "especially associated with the wilder sort of evening parties . . . and with the ecstatic dancing practised in the Dionysiac and similar cults." In the *Republic* (399d), Socrates excludes it from the guardians' education on the grounds that, since it can imitate all modes (*harmoniai*), it is used to imitate both good and bad characters and tempers.

122. Originally choral odes to Dionysus, dithyrambs underwent considerable evolution over the years. The best-known composers of dithyrambs from the earlier (than, e.g., Cinesias's) generation were Simonides, Pindar, and Bacchylides.

123. *Semnos* means revered, august, holy, solemn, pompous. Often ironic in Plato, I have most often rendered it "solemn."

502c CAL.: This at least is clear, Socrates—that it strives rather for pleasure and gratifying the spectators.

SOC.: And were we just now saying, Callicles, that such a thing is flattery?

CAL.: Certainly.

SOC.: Come then, if someone stripped off the tune, rhythm, and meter from every poetic composition, would what is left turn out to be anything other than speeches?

CAL.: Necessarily so.

SOC.: So are these speeches then spoken before a big mob and before the people?

CAL.: I say so.

SOC.: The poetic art, therefore, is a certain popular speaking.

502d CAL.: So it appears.

SOC.: Would it then be a rhetorical popular speaking? Or don't the poets seem to you to speak rhetorically in the theaters?

CAL.: They seem to, to me.

SOC.: Now therefore we have found a certain rhetoric directed toward such a people as consists of children together with women and men, both slave and free—a rhetoric that we do not altogether admire, for we assert that it is a flattering one.

CAL.: Certainly.

SOC.: So be it. Now what about the rhetoric directed toward the Athe-
502e nian people and the other peoples of free men in the cities—what in the world is it, in our view? Do the rhetors in your opinion always speak with a view to the best, aiming at this, that because of their speeches the citizens shall be as good as possible? Or do these men too strive for gratifying the citizens and, for the sake of their own private interest, make light of the common interest, and associate with the peoples as if with children, trying only to gratify them, and giving no
503a heed to whether they will be better or worse because of these things?

CAL.: What you are asking now is no longer simple: for there are some who care about the citizens when they say what they say, and there are also such as you say.

SOC.: That is enough. For if this thing too[124] is double, one part of it anyway would be flattery and shameful popular speaking, and the

124. The "too" would have to refer back, it seems, to the twofold arts-flatteries set forth earlier; understanding *kai* differently (as Dodds suggests) would yield the meaning "if this thing is indeed double."

other would be noble: making preparations for the citizens' souls to be as good as possible and fighting to say the best things, whether

503b they will be more pleasant or more unpleasant to the hearers. But this rhetoric you have never yet seen; or if you can mention one of the rhetors as such, why haven't you declared to me too who he is?

CAL.: But by Zeus I cannot mention anyone for you—not of the current rhetors, at any rate.

SOC.: What then? Can you mention one of the ancients through whom the Athenians, worse at an earlier time, are judged to have become better, after he began to practice popular speaking? For I do not know who this man is.

503c CAL.: What? Do you not hear that Themistocles turned out to be a good man, and Cimon, and Miltiades, and Pericles himself, who recently came to his end, whom you too have heard?[125]

SOC.: If, at any rate, Callicles, true virtue is what you were saying earlier—satisfying both one's own and others' desires. But if it is not this, but what we were compelled to agree in the subsequent argument—to fulfill those desires that, when sated, make a human being

503d better, but not those that make him worse (and this would be a certain art)—then I, for one, don't know how I could mention anyone of these as such a man.

CAL.: But if you do a fine job of seeking, you will find.[126]

SOC.: Then let's examine it in this calm manner and see if anyone of these turned out to be such a one. Well then, won't the good man,

503e who speaks with a view to the best, say what he says not at random but looking off toward something? Just as all the other craftsmen look toward their work when each chooses and applies what he applies, not at random, but in order that he can get this thing he is working on to have a certain form. For example, if you wish to look

---

125. Gorgias had earlier mentioned Themistocles and Pericles; see note at 455e. Pericles died in the second year of the Peloponnesian War, 429 B.C. Miltiades led the Athenian troops that won the great victory in the first Persian War at Marathon in 490. His son, Cimon, worked with Aristides (see 526b) to found the Delian League (forerunner to the Athenian Empire) in the latter stages of the second Persian War, 478–477; he was opposed by the more democratic party (led eventually by Pericles).

126. Various editors deal variously with problems in the manuscripts here, regarding both what is said and who says it. I have followed Burnet's version (J. Burnet, *Platonis Opera* [Oxford Classical Text], vol. 3 [Oxford: Clarendon Press, 1903]. Dodds argues for a different emendation, which would yield this: "SOC.: . . . (and this seemed to us to be a certain art)— Can you say that some one of these was such a man?—CAL.: I, for one, don't know how I could say so.—SOC.: But if you do a fine job of seeking, you will find. Then let's examine it. . . ."

at painters, house builders, shipwrights, all the other craftsmen—whomever of them you wish—see how each man puts down each thing that he puts down into a certain arrangement, and furthermore

504a compels one thing to fit and harmonize with another, until he has composed the whole as an arranged and ordered thing. And indeed the other craftsmen, and those concerned with the body, of whom we were just now speaking, trainers and doctors—they order the body, I suppose, and arrange it together. Do we agree that this is so or not?

CAL.: Let this be so.

SOC.: Then a house that happened to have arrangement and order would be useful, and one lacking arrangement would be degenerate?

CAL.: I say so.

SOC.: And the same way for a ship too?

504b CAL.: Yes.

SOC.: Now, do we say so about our bodies as well?

CAL.: Certainly.

SOC.: And what about the soul? Will it be useful when it happens to have lack of arrangement, or arrangement and a certain order?

CAL.: From what preceded, it is necessary to agree on this too.

SOC.: What then is the name of that which, in the body, comes into being from arrangement and order?

CAL.: You probably mean health and strength.

504c SOC.: I do. And now, in turn, what about that which arises within the soul from arrangement and order? Try to find and state the name, just as for the former case.

CAL.: Why don't you say it yourself, Socrates?

SOC.: Well, if that's more pleasant for you, I shall say. And if in your opinion I speak finely, say yes, and if not, refute and don't yield. For in my opinion the body's arrangements have the name "the healthy," from which health comes into being in it, and the rest of the body's virtue. Are these things so or not?

CAL.: They are.

504d SOC.: The soul's arrangements and orderings, on the other hand, have (in my opinion) the name "the lawful" and "law," whence they become both lawful and orderly; and these things are justice and moderation. Do you say yes or no?

CAL.: Let it be.

SOC.: That rhetor, then—the artful and good one—will look toward these things, when he applies to souls both the speeches that he speaks and all actions; and when he gives something as a gift, he will give it, and when he takes something away, he will take it away, al-

504e ways directing his mind toward how he may get justice to come into being in the citizens' souls and injustice to be removed, moderation to arise within and intemperance to be removed, the rest of virtue to arise within and badness to depart. Do you grant it or not?

CAL.: I grant it.

SOC.: Indeed what advantage is there, Callicles, in giving to a sick body in a degenerate condition either much and the most pleasant food, or drink, or anything else, which would benefit him not a bit more, or indeed to the contrary, according to the just argument, even less? Are these things so?

505a CAL.: Let them be so.

SOC.: For I do not think it profits a human being to live with a degenerate condition of body; for in this way he must necessarily live degenerately too. Or isn't it so?

CAL.: Yes.

SOC.: And so then doctors for the most part allow a healthy man to satisfy his desires, such as when hungry to eat as much as he wishes or when thirsty to drink, but they never, one might almost say, allow a sick man to fill up on the things he desires. Do you too grant this?

CAL.: I do.

505b SOC.: And does not the same way, best of men, hold as regards the soul? As long as it is base—being thoughtless, intemperate, unjust, and impious—one must keep it away from desires and not permit it to do any other things than those from which it will be better. Do you say yes or no?

CAL.: Yes, I say.

SOC.: For thus, I suppose, it's better for the soul itself.

CAL.: Certainly.

SOC.: Now then, is keeping it away from the things it desires punishing?

CAL.: Yes.

SOC.: Being punished, therefore, is better for the soul than intemperance,[127] as you were thinking just now.

505c CAL.: I don't know what you are saying, Socrates, so ask someone else.

---

127. On the relation of these words *kolazesthai*, to be punished, and *akolasia*, intemperance, see note at 476a.

soc.: This man here does not abide being benefited and suffering for himself this thing that the argument is about, being punished.

cal.: Nor do I care at all about the things you are saying, and I answered you these things as a favor to Gorgias.[128]

soc.: So be it. What then shall we do? Are we breaking off the argument in the middle?

cal.: You yourself will know.

soc.: Well, they say that it is not righteous[129] to abandon even myths
505d in the middle, but one must put a head on, so that it not go around without a head. So answer the remaining things too, so that our argument may get a head.

cal.: How violent you are, Socrates. But if you're persuaded by me, you'll bid this argument farewell,[130] or else you'll converse with someone else.

soc.: Who else is willing then? Let us not abandon the argument there, incomplete.

cal.: Couldn't you go through the argument yourself, either speaking by yourself or answering yourself?

505e soc.: So that Epicharmus's saying may come to pass for me: "What two men were saying beforehand, I, being one," may become sufficient for.[131] Yet it may well be most necessary. Now then let's do it this way; I, at any rate, think we all must be lovers of victory in regard to knowing what is the true and what is falsehood as regards the things we are talking about. For it is a common good for all that it become
506a manifest. I shall therefore go through in speech how it seems to me to be; and if I seem to any one of you to agree with myself on things that are not, you must take me up on it and refute. For I, at any rate, do not say what I say with knowledge,[132] but I am seeking in common with you—so that, if one who disputes me is manifestly saying something, I shall be the first to grant it. I say these things, however,

---

128. *Charin* with a genitive is a standard way of saying "for someone's sake." But *charis* means grace, pleasure, gratitude, favor; it is the root of *charizesthai*, "to gratify," and *chairein*, "to rejoice." Here Callicles is gratifying not himself but Gorgias.

129. *Themis*, see second note at 497c.

130. A more literal translation of *eaō auto chairein*, "bid it farewell," would be "let it rejoice"; see the first note at 505c.

131. Epicharmus, a Sicilian writer of nonchoral comedies, is mentioned as the consummate poet of comedy in Plato's *Theaetetus* 152e.

132. Dodds accepts here the words *panu ti* found in one manuscript; the translation might then be: "with quite complete knowledge."

if it seems that the argument should be carried through to a conclusion; but if you don't wish it, then let's bid it farewell and go away.

GOR.: But it doesn't seem to me, Socrates, that we should go away yet;
506b rather, you should finish going through the argument. And it appears to me that it seems so to the others too. I myself, in any case, wish to hear you go through the remaining things by yourself.

SOC.: Well certainly, Gorgias, I myself too—I would with pleasure have gone on talking with Callicles here, until I had given him back the speech of Amphion for the speech of Zethus. But since you, Callicles, are not willing to join in carrying through the argument to a
506c conclusion, then listen to me and interrupt, if something I say does not seem fine to you. And if you thoroughly refute me, I shall not be annoyed with you as you were with me, but you will be inscribed with me as the greatest benefactor.

CAL.: Speak, good man, and finish it yourself.

SOC.: Then listen to me take up the argument from the beginning. Are the pleasant and the good the same thing? No, not the same, as Callicles and I agreed. Must the pleasant be done for the sake of the good or the good for the sake of the pleasant? The pleasant for the sake
506d of the good. And is the pleasant this thing through which we are pleased, when it comes to be present; and is the good that through which we are good, when it is present? Certainly. But surely we are good—both we and all other things that are good—when some virtue comes to be present? It seems necessary to me, Callicles. Now then, the virtue of each thing—of implement, body, soul too, and every living being[133]—does not come to be present in the finest manner simply at random, but by arrangement, correctness, and art, which has been assigned to each of them; are these things so? I say
506e yes. Then is the virtue of each thing something that has been arranged and ordered by arrangement? I should say so. Is it therefore a certain order arising in each thing—each thing's own order—that makes each of the beings good? It seems so to me, at least. Then is a soul too that has its own order better than a disordered one? Necessarily. And surely the one that has order is orderly? How would it not be? And
507a the orderly one is moderate? Very necessarily. The moderate soul is therefore good. I don't have any other things to say against these, Callicles my friend; but if you do, teach us.

CAL.: Speak, good man.

---

133. Or one could translate "every animal."

soc.: I say, then, that if the moderate soul is good, the one that suffers the opposite to the moderate is bad; and this would be the foolish and intemperate soul.[134] Certainly. And surely the moderate man would do fitting things concerning both gods and human beings;
507b for he who does unfitting things would not show moderation. These things are necessarily so. And surely he who does fitting things concerning human beings would do just things; and concerning gods, pious things; and he who does just and pious things must of necessity be just and pious. These things are so. And indeed, of necessity, courageous as well. For it is not the part of a moderate man either to pursue or to flee things that are not fitting, but to flee and to pursue what he ought—affairs, human beings, pleasures, and pains—and to
507c abide and be steadfast wherever he ought. So it is very necessary, Callicles, that the moderate man as we have described him, since he is just, courageous, and pious, must be the completely good man; and the good man must do what he does well and nobly; and the man who does well must be blessed and happy, while the base man who does badly must be wretched. And this would be the one in an opposite condition to the moderate men—the intemperate man, whom you were praising.

I therefore lay down these things in this way and I assert that they
507d are true. And if they are true, he who wishes to be happy must, it would seem, pursue and practice moderation, and each of us must flee intemperance as fast as his feet will carry him; and one must most of all prepare to have no need of punishment, but if oneself or some other of one's own—whether private man or city—needs it, one must apply the just penalty and punish, if he is to be happy. This in my opinion is the goal looking toward which one must live, straining to direct all one's own and the city's things toward this, that jus-
507e tice and moderation will be present for him who is to be blessed; thus must one act, not allowing desires to be intemperate and striving to satiate them—an endless evil, living a robber's life. For such a one would be dear friend neither to another human being nor to god; for he would be unable to share in common, and he in whom there is no community would not have friendship. The wise[135] say, Callicles, that
508a heaven, earth, gods, and human beings are held together by com-

134. *Sōphrōn,* "moderate," has a wide range of meanings: temperate, self-controlled, of sound mind, sensible; hence Socrates here proposes two opposites.
135. Dodds argues persuasively that the scholiast and Olympiodorus correctly identify these wise men as Pythagoreans.

munity, friendship, orderliness, moderation, and justness; and on account of these things, comrade, they call this whole an order,[136] not disorder and intemperance. You, however, seem to me not to turn your mind to these things, wise though you are about them, but it has escaped your notice that geometrical equality[137] has great power among both gods and human beings, whereas you think one must practice taking more; for you have no care for geometry. So be it:

508b   either this argument must be refuted for us, to show that it is not by the possession of justice and moderation that the happy are happy and by the possession of evil that the wretched are wretched; or else if this argument is true, we must examine what the consequences are. All those earlier things follow, Callicles, upon which you asked me if I was speaking seriously, when I said that one must accuse oneself, one's son, and one's comrade, if he is doing an injustice, and one must use rhetoric for this. And the things you thought Polus granted because of shame were therefore true, that doing injustice is as much

508c   worse than suffering injustice as it is more shameful; and he who is to be correctly rhetorical must therefore be just and a knower of the just things, which in turn Polus said Gorgias agreed to through shame.

These things being so, let us examine what in the world it is that you reproach me for and whether what is said is fine or not: that I am unable, then, to help either myself or anyone of my friends or relatives, or to save them from the greatest dangers, but am at the mercy of whoever wishes, just as those without civic rights[138] are at the

508d   mercy of whoever wants—whether he wishes to strike me a crack on the jaw (to use this youthful phrase from your speech), to take away my possessions, to expel me from the city, or—the ultimate—to kill me; and to be in this condition is of all things most shameful, as your argument goes. But my argument now—while it has already been said many times, nothing prevents its being said again as well: I deny, Callicles, that being unjustly struck a crack on the jaw is most

508e   shameful, or having my body or my purse cut; rather, striking and cutting me and my things unjustly is more shameful and worse; and

136. *Kosmos.*
137. Such is a literal translation; we would tend to say "proportionate equality" or "proportionality." Aristotle develops this notion in detail to describe distributive justice (*Nicomachean Ethics* 5.1131a10–b22).
138. This word, *atimos*, was translated "unhonored" at 486c; see note there.

for that matter stealing, enslaving, housebreaking, and in short doing any injustice whatsoever to me and my things is both worse and more shameful for him who does injustice than for me who suffer injustice. These things, above there in the earlier arguments, manifestly appeared to us in this way that I am saying, and they are held down

509a and bound—if it is possible to say something rather rude—with iron and adamantine arguments, as it would seem, at any rate; and if you (or someone more youthful than you) do not loosen them, he who says something different from what I am now saying won't be able to say anything fine. For my speech is always the same: I do not know how these things are, but of those people I fall in with, as now, no one who says something different is able not to be ridiculous. So

509b then, again, I put it that these things are so. And if so, and the greatest of evils is injustice for the doer of injustice and a still greater evil than this greatest one—if that's possible—is for the doer of injustice not to pay the just penalty, what help would it be, for not being able to provide himself with which, a human being would be ridiculous in truth? Would it not be that one which turns the greatest harm away from us? It is very necessary that this be the most shameful help not to be able to provide for oneself or for one's friends and relatives; sec-

509c ond would be help against the second evil, third against the third, and so on. As the greatness of each evil naturally is, so too is the nobility of being able to help against each and the shame of not being able. Is it otherwise or thus, Callicles?

CAL.: Not otherwise.

SOC.: Then of these two, doing injustice and suffering it, we assert that doing injustice is the greater evil, suffering injustice the lesser.

509d By preparing what, then, would a human being help himself, so as to have both of these benefits—that of not doing injustice and that of not suffering injustice? Is it power or wish? This is how I mean it: if he does not wish to suffer injustice, will he not suffer injustice; or if he has prepared a power of not suffering injustice, will he not suffer injustice?

CAL.: This at least is clear: it is if he has prepared power.

SOC.: Now what about doing injustice? If he does not wish to do in-

509e justice, is this sufficient—for he will not do injustice—or against this thing too must one prepare a certain power and art, as he will do injustice if he does not learn and practice them? Why haven't you answered me this very thing, Callicles? Were Polus and I in your opinion correctly compelled in the earlier speeches to agree, or were we not, when we agreed that no one does injustice wishing to do so, but all doers of injustice do so involuntarily?

510a CAL.: Let this be so for you, Socrates, so that you may bring the argument to a conclusion.

soc.: One must therefore prepare a certain power and art against this too, as it would seem, in order that we not do injustice.

CAL.: Certainly.

soc.: What in the world, then, is the art for the preparation of suffering no injustice or as little as possible? Examine if it seems to you what it does to me. For to me, it seems to be the following: one must either rule in the city oneself—or even rule as tyrant—or else be a comrade of the existing regime.[139]

CAL.: Do you see, Socrates, how ready I am to praise, if something 510b you say is fine? This thing you have said is altogether fine in my opinion.

soc.: Now consider whether the following thing I say seems good to you too. In my opinion, each man is the friend of another to the greatest possible degree, who the ancient and wise said was the friend: like to like. Doesn't it seem so to you too?

CAL.: It does to me.

soc.: So then, where a savage and uneducated tyrant is ruler, if someone in the city is much better than this man, the tyrant I suppose 510c would fear him, and he could never become this man's[140] friend with his whole mind.

CAL.: These things are so.

soc.: Nor, if someone were much lowlier, would he; for the tyrant would despise him and would never be serious about him as toward a friend.

CAL.: These things are also true.

soc.: As friend of such a one, then, there remains worth speaking of

---

139. *Politeia*, "regime" or political system or constitution (the title of Plato's *Republic*), for Plato as for Aristotle is chiefly determined by who rules. *Hetairos*, which has the broad meaning "comrade," companion, friend, has also the specific meaning of political partisan, fellow member of a political faction or party.

140. That is, the tyrant's. There is some difficulty here and in the next exchange as to whether *houtos* ("this man") refers to the tyrant or the other, and whether *philos* ("friend") has the active ("friend") sense or the passive (dear, object of friendship). An alternative interpretation would be "and [the tyrant] could never become this man's friend with his whole mind."

only that man who, being of the same character and praising and blaming the same things, is willing to be ruled and to be submissive
510d to the ruler. This man will have great power in that city; to this man no one will rejoice to do injustice. Isn't this how it is?

CAL.: Yes.

SOC.: Then if some one of the young in that city thought, "In what way might I have great power, and no one might do me an injustice?" this, it would seem, is the path for him: immediately from youth to accustom himself to rejoice and to be distressed at the same things as the master, and to make preparations so as to be as much as possible like that man. Isn't it so?

CAL.: Yes.

SOC.: So for this man, then, not suffering injustice and having great
510e power (as your argument goes) in the city will have been accomplished.

CAL.: Certainly.

SOC.: Will not doing injustice, then, be accomplished too? Or far from it, if he is like the ruler who is unjust and if he has great power alongside this man? Wholly to the contrary, I think at any rate, in this way his preparation will be aimed at being able to do as much injustice as possible and not to pay the just penalty when he does it. Won't it?

CAL.: It appears so.

511a SOC.: So then the greatest evil will befall him, when he is degenerate and maimed in his soul through imitation of the master and through power.

CAL.: I don't know how you twist the arguments up and down each time, Socrates. Or don't you know that this man who imitates will kill that one who does not imitate, if he wishes, and confiscate his property?

511b SOC.: I know, good Callicles, unless I'm deaf—since I hear you and just now Polus many times and almost all others in the city; but you now hear from me: that he will kill, if he wishes, but it will be a base man killing a noble and good one.

CAL.: Isn't this exactly the infuriating thing?

SOC.: Not for him who has intelligence, as the argument indicates. Or do you think a human being ought to make preparations for living as
511c long a time as possible and to practice those arts that always save us from dangers—like the one you are bidding me to practice, rhetoric that brings us through safely in the law courts?

CAL.: Yes, by Zeus, and I'm counseling you correctly!

SOC.: What about this, you best of men? Does the science of swimming seem to you to be an august one?

CAL.: No, by Zeus! Not to me, at any rate.

SOC.: And yet it too saves human beings from death, when they fall into something of the sort where this science is needed. But if this one

511d   seems to you to be small, I shall speak to you of one greater than this, the pilot's art, which saves not only souls[141] but also bodies and possessions from the ultimate dangers, just as rhetoric does. And this art is unostentatious and orderly, and does not assume an august bearing[142] on the grounds that it accomplishes something splendid. But, having accomplished the same things as the forensic art,[143] if it saves you coming hither from Aegina, it demands two obols, I think;

511e   and if from Egypt or the Pontus, for this great benefaction, having saved all that I was speaking of just now—oneself, children, possessions, and womenfolk—disembarking them in the harbor, it demands at the very most two drachmas. And the man himself who has the art and has accomplished these things, stepping off alongside the sea and the ship, walks around with a modest bearing. For he knows, I think, how to calculate that it is unclear which ones of those sailing with him he has benefited by not letting them be thrown into the sea

512a   and which ones he has harmed, knowing that he disembarked them no better than what they were like when they embarked, in respect to either their bodies or their souls. He therefore calculates thus: if someone possessed by great and incurable sicknesses of the body has not drowned, this man is wretched not to have died and has received no benefit from him; it therefore cannot be that, if someone has many incurable sicknesses in what is held in higher honor than the body, the soul, this man should live and he the pilot will help him by sav-

512b   ing him either from the sea or from a law court or from any other place whatsoever. Rather, he knows that it is not better for the degenerate human being to live, for he must necessarily live badly.

141. We would normally say "lives," of course. As the principle of life, *psuchē* can sometimes mean being alive or life.

142. Irwin's note points out that some terms used here remind of the description of non-arts like cosmetic (464c, 465b) and apply with particular propriety to "an elaborate, figurative rhetorical style" (Terence Irwin, *Plato; Gorgias* [Translated with Notes] [Oxford: Clarendon Press, 1979].

143. *Dikanikē*, similar to but perhaps with more contemptuous overtones (as at *Republic* 405a) than *dikastikē*, "the judge's art" at 520b.

For these reasons it is not the convention for the pilot to affect an august air, even though he saves us, nor, you amazing man, for the engineer,[144] who can sometimes save us no less than the general, not to mention the pilot, or anyone else; for there are times when he saves whole cities. He does not seem to you to be on the level of the forensic speaker? Yet if he wished, Callicles, to say the things that you
512c   do, making his business out to be august, he would bury you with speeches, saying and exhorting that you must become engineers, since the other things are nothing; for he would have a sufficient argument. But you nonetheless despise him and his art, and you would label him an engineer as if in reproach, and you would not be willing to give your daughter to his son or yourself to take his daughter for your son. Yet on the basis of the things for which you praise your own affairs, by what just argument do you despise the engineer and
512d   the others of whom I was speaking just now? I know that you would say you are better and of better ancestry. But if the better is not what I say, but virtue is simply this, saving oneself and one's own property—of whatever sort one happens to be—your blame of the engineer, of the doctor, and of all the other arts that have been produced for the sake of saving us, becomes ridiculous. But, you blessed man, see if the noble[145] and the good are not something other than saving and being saved. For the true man, at any rate, must reject living any
512e   amount of time whatsoever, and must not be a lover of life.[146] Rather, turning over what concerns these things to the god and believing the women's saying that no man may escape his destiny, he must investigate what comes after this: In what way may he who is going to live
513a   for a time live best? Is it by making himself like that regime in which he lives, and should you therefore now become as much as possible like the Athenian people, if you are to be dear friend to it and to have great power in the city? See if this is profitable for you and for me, you demonic man, so that we shall not suffer what they say the Thessalian women who draw down the moon suffer: our choice of this power in the city will be at the cost of the things dearest to us.[147] And

144. *Mēchanopoios:* more literally, "maker of devices."
145. *Gennaios,* usually translated "nobly born."
146. Literally, "of soul"; see first note at 511d.
147. Thessaly, an area of Greece north of Attica, was considered an area especially endowed with witches. Witches, it was believed, often paid for the acquisition of their power through losing a family member or some faculty, like sight.

if you think any human being at all will impart to you a certain art
513b   such as to make you have great power in this city while being unlike
the regime, whether for better or for worse, as it seems to me, you are
not taking counsel correctly, Callicles. For you must be not an imitator but like these men in your very own nature, if you are to achieve
something genuine in friendship with the Athenian people—and
yes, by Zeus, with the son of Pyrilampes to boot! So then, whoever
will turn you out most like these men will make you skilled in politics and in rhetoric, as you desire to be skilled in politics. For each
513c   group of men rejoice at speeches said in accord with their own character and are annoyed at those of an alien character—unless you
say something else, dear head.[148] Do we say anything against these
things, Callicles?

CAL.: In some way, I don't know what, what you say seems good to
me, Socrates; but I suffer the experience of the many—I am not altogether persuaded by you.

SOC.: Yes, for love[149] of the people, Callicles, which is present in your
soul, opposes me. But if we investigate these same things often and
513d   better, perhaps you will be persuaded.[150] Well then, remember that
we said there are two means of preparing for taking care of each
thing, body and soul: one associates with the one for the sake of pleasure, with the other for the sake of the best, not yielding as a favor but
fighting. Weren't these the things we were defining then?

CAL.: Certainly.

SOC.: The one aiming at pleasure, then, happens to be ignoble and
nothing other than flattery; isn't it?

513e   CAL.: Let it be so for you, if you wish.

SOC.: And is the other's aim that what we are taking care of, whether
it happens to be body or soul, shall be as good as possible?[151]

CAL.: Certainly.

---

148. On this curious mode of address, see *Phaedrus* 234d and note there.

149. The word is *erōs*; the related verb (participial form) was used in 481d. Elsewhere in
this dialogue, words involving "love" have translated *phil-* (e.g., "love of victory" at 457e).
In the *Phaedrus,* where *erōs* is much discussed, I have also used "love" and indicated with
footnotes where "love" translates one of the *phil-* words.

150. The manuscripts have the adverb *isōs*, "perhaps," oddly placed in this sentence. I follow Ast and others in moving it. Dodds considers it a gloss; if that is correct, one must
drop the softening "perhaps" from Socrates' assertion.

151. Arguing that this adds nothing to what was already agreed to at d4; Dodds proposes
the addition of *gennaiotera* so that the sentence would read: "Is the other one nobler,
whose aim is. . . ."

soc.: Must we therefore put our hand to the city and the citizens in this way, to take care of them, making the citizens themselves as good as possible? For surely without this, as we found earlier, there
514a is no advantage in applying any other benefaction, unless the understanding of those who are going to get either many possessions or rule over others or any other power is noble and good. Should we put it that this is the case?

cal.: Certainly, if it's more pleasant for you.

soc.: Then if, Callicles, intending to act publicly in political affairs, we urged each other on to building—to the greatest buildings, whether of walls or dockyards or sacred temples—would we have to examine ourselves and inquire first whether we know the art or do
514b not know it, that is, the art of building, and from whom we learned it? Would we have to do this or not?

cal.: Certainly.

soc.: So would this in turn be second: whether we have ever built any building privately, either for someone of our friends or our own, and whether this building is beautiful or ugly? And if we consider
514c and find that our teachers have been good and well spoken of, and that many beautiful buildings have been built by us with our teachers and many private buildings by us after we left our teachers— these being our circumstances, it would belong to us, as people who have intelligence, to proceed to public works. But if we could display no teacher of ours, and either no building or many worthless ones, surely thus it would be foolish, I suppose, to put our hand to public works and urge each other on to these. Should we assert that these
514d are correct statements or not?

cal.: Certainly.

soc.: Then is this how it is for all things? For example, if, putting our hand to public practice, we urged each other on as being adequate doctors, I suppose I should examine you and you me: "Well then, by the gods, what is the bodily condition of Socrates himself in regard to health? Or has anyone else yet been released from sickness by Socrates, whether slave or free?" And I think I should consider other things of this sort about you. And if we found no one who had be-
514e come better in regard to his body because of us—neither foreigner nor townsman, neither man nor woman—by Zeus, Callicles, would it not in truth be ridiculous for human beings to proceed so far in folly as, before making many things in private practice however we

happen to, correcting many, and exercising ourselves adequately in the art, to attempt to learn pottery on the wine jar, as this saying goes,[152] and to attempt to be in public practice ourselves and urge on other men of this sort? Would it not seem to you to be thoughtless to act thus?

CAL.: It would to me.

515a SOC.: Now then, you best of men, since you are yourself just now beginning to do the city's business and urge me on and reproach me for not doing it, shall we not examine each other: "Well then, has Callicles yet made anyone of the citizens better? Is there someone who was base before—unjust, intemperate, and foolish—and has become noble and good because of Callicles—whether foreigner or townsman,
515b slave or free?" Tell me, if someone questions you closely about these things, Callicles, what will you say? What human being will you say you have made better through intercourse with you? Do you shrink from answering, if indeed there is some work of yours, while you are still a private man, before you put your hand to public practice?

CAL.: You are a lover of victory, Socrates.

SOC.: But I am not asking from love of victory, but truly wishing to know what in the world is the way you think you ought to act in pol-
515c itics among us. Can it be that, as you enter upon the city's business, you will then take care of anything else for us but that we citizens be as good as possible? Or have we not agreed many times already that the political man must do this? Have we agreed or not? Answer! We have agreed—I shall answer for you. Accordingly, if this is what the good man must prepare for his own city, remember now and tell me whether those men of whom you were speaking a little earlier still
515d seem to you to have been good citizens—Pericles, Cimon, Miltiades, and Themistocles.

CAL.: They do to me.

SOC.: So if indeed they were good, then it is clear that each of them made the citizens better instead of worse. Did they do so or not?

CAL.: Yes.

SOC.: So then, when Pericles began to speak in the people's assembly, were the Athenians worse than when he made his final speeches?

CAL.: Perhaps.

152. A wine jar was a large and difficult work of pottery; the beginner should start with smaller and simpler objects. Socrates refers to this same saying in the *Laches* at 187b, in a context involving education of the young.

soc.: There is no "perhaps" about it, best of men, but a necessity, from the things agreed on, if indeed that man was a good citizen.

515e cal.: So what of it?

soc.: Nothing; but in addition to this tell me the following, if the Athenians are said to have become better because of Pericles, or, quite the opposite, to have been corrupted by him. For I at any rate hear these things, that Pericles made the Athenians lazy, cowardly, babbling, and money lovers, when he first brought them into the state of mercenaries.[153]

cal.: You hear these things, Socrates, from the men with cauliflower ears.[154]

soc.: But the following things are no longer what I hear, but what I distinctly know, and you do too: that at first Pericles was well reputed, and the Athenians voted no shameful judgment in condemnation of him, at the time when they were worse. But after they had

516a become noble and good through him, toward the end of Pericles' life, they voted a condemnation of him for theft, and came close to sentencing him to death, clearly on the grounds that he was base.[155]

cal.: So what? Was Pericles bad on account of this?

soc.: A caretaker of asses, horses, or oxen, at any rate, who was of this sort, would seem to be bad, if when he took them over, they neither kicked nor butted not bit him, but then he brought them forth doing

516b all these things through savageness. Or doesn't any caretaker whatsoever of any animal whatsoever seem to you to be bad who, having taken them over gentler, brings them forth more savage than he took them over? Does it seem so or not?

cal.: Certainly, so that I may gratify you.

soc.: Now then gratify me by answering this too: is a human being too one of the animals or not?

cal.: How could he not be?

soc.: Well then, did Pericles take care of human beings?

---

153. Pericles introduced payment for service on juries and the council (also pay for soldiers and sailors), thus making the Athenian regime more democratic.

154. "Cauliflower ears" is Dodds's translation; more literally, "with broken ears." Certain aristocratic or oligarchic Athenians affected a pro-Spartan taste, which included fondness for boxing and the like. See Socrates' discussion at *Protagoras* 342b.

155. The ironical rhetorical tone of this indictment should perhaps remind us of Polus's earlier indictment of Archelaus. The accounts in Thucydides and Plutarch suggest that Socrates exaggerates here, and Socrates does not mention that the Athenians repented soon after and restored Pericles to office (Thucydides 2.65.4).

CAL.: Yes.

SOC.: What then? Shouldn't they, as we recently agreed, have become
516c   more just instead of more unjust through him, if indeed he took care
of them as someone good in political affairs?

CAL.: Certainly.

SOC.: Well then, are the just gentle, as Homer said?[156] What do you
say? Not so?

CAL.: Yes.

SOC.: But surely he showed them forth more savage than they were
when he took them over—and that against himself, against whom he
would have wished it least.

CAL.: Do you wish that I agree with you?

SOC.: If, that is, the things I'm saying seem true to you.

CAL.: Then let them be so.

SOC.: So, if more savage, then more unjust and worse?

516d   CAL.: Let it be so.

SOC.: Therefore Pericles was not good in political affairs, from this
argument.

CAL.: You, at any rate, say not.

SOC.: By Zeus, so do you, from the things you agree on! But tell me
once more about Cimon. Didn't these men he was caring for ostra-
cize him, so that they would not hear his voice for ten years?[157] And
didn't they do these same things to Themistocles, and add on the
516e   penalty of exile? And didn't they vote to throw Miltiades, of Marathon fame, into the pit, and were it not for the president,[158] he would
have fallen in? And yet if these men were good, as you assert, they
would never have suffered these things. It cannot be, can it, that good
charioteers in the beginning do not fall from the chariots, but that
when they have cared for the horses and have themselves become
better charioteers, then they fall out? These things are not so either in
chariot driving or in any other work; or does it seem so to you?

156. On several occasions (e.g., *Odyssey* 6.120) Homer uses the phrase *hubristai te kai agrioi
oude dikaioi*, "wanton and savage and not just" as opposed to loving strangers and being of
god-fearing mind. (On *hubris*, wanton outrage, see *Phaedrus* 238a.)
157. Ostracism was not even supposed necessarily to result from misconduct. (The most
notorious example of unjust ostracism is doubtless that of Aristides the Just.) Cimon was
ostracized in 461 after an unsuccessful attempt to intervene in Sparta's Messenian War.
According to Plutarch's *Life of Cimon* 17, he was recalled soon afterwards.
158. *Pyrtanis.* At 473e Socrates referred to his tribe as presiding; this president's success in
saving Miltiades contrasts with Socrates' failure to save the generals after Arginusae.

CAL.: Not to me.

517a   SOC.: The earlier arguments, therefore, were true, it would appear, that we know no one in this city who has become a good man in political affairs.[159] You agree that there is no one among those of today, and moreover from the earlier ones you pick out these men; but they have been plainly revealed to be equal to those of today, so that if these men were rhetors, they used neither the true[160] art of rhetoric— or they would not have fallen out—nor the flattering one.

CAL.: But it is nevertheless far from being the case, Socrates, that any-
517b   one of those today has ever accomplished such works as anyone you wish of these men has accomplished.

SOC.: You demonic man, I don't blame these men either—that is, not in their being servants of the city; indeed in my opinion they became more skilled in service than those of today, at any rate, and more capable of supplying the city with the things it desired. But as to leading desires in a different direction and not yielding, persuading and forcing them toward the condition in which the citizens were to be
517c   better, those earlier men excelled these in nothing, one might almost say; yet this is the one work of a good citizen. But I agree with you that those earlier men were more terribly clever than these at supplying ships, walls, dockyards, and many other such things. You and I, then, are doing a laughable thing in the arguments; for in the whole time that we have been conversing, we haven't stopped always being carried around to the same thing and ignoring what we are, each of us, saying. So I think, at any rate, you have many times agreed and un-
517d   derstood that this occupation concerned both with the body and with the soul is indeed a certain double one, and that the one is skilled in service, by which it is possible to supply food if our bodies are hungry, drink if they are thirsty, clothing, bedding, and shoes if they are cold, and other things for which bodies come into a state of desire. And I speak to you on purpose through the same likenesses, so that you may thoroughly understand more easily. For the one skilled at supplying these things is either the retailer or importer or craftsman
517e   of some one of these same things—baker, cook, weaver, cobbler, or

159. In the *Meno* (93a), by contrast, Socrates asserts that in his opinion Athens has had men good in political affairs; he uses as examples Themistocles, Aristides, and Pericles. Socrates cites Pericles as wise in political matters in the *Protagoras* (320a) and as perhaps the most perfect of rhetors in the *Phaedrus* (269e–270b).
160. Or truthful, *alēthinos;* cf. the true (or truthful) city in the *Republic* 372e.

leather dresser. Being of such a sort, it is nothing amazing that he seems, to himself and to the others, to be the caretaker of the body, and thus to everyone who does not know that besides all these there is a certain gymnastic and medical art, which is really the care for the body and which fittingly rules all these arts and uses their works, be- cause of its knowing what is useful and base among foods or drinks 518a for the body's virtue, while all these others are ignorant. It is for this reason that these other arts are slavish, servile, and illiberal as regards their occupation with the body, and the gymnastic art and medical art are, in accordance with what is just, mistresses of these. Well then, at one time you seem to me to understand that these same things in fact obtain for the soul as well, when I am saying so, and you agree as if you know what I mean; but a little later you come along and say that 518b there have been human beings who were noble and good citizens in the city, and when I ask who, you seem to me to put forward, con- cerning political affairs, human beings of a very similar sort as if, when I asked about gymnastic matters who have been or are good caretakers of bodies, you said to me in all seriousness that these men, Thearion the baker, Mithaicus who has written on Sicilian cookery, and Sarambus the retailer, have been amazing caretakers of bodies— 518c one preparing amazing loaves, another food, and the other wine.

So perhaps you would become infuriated if I said to you: "Human being, you understand nothing about gymnastic. You are telling me of human beings who are servants and provisioners of desires but understand nothing noble and good about them. If so they happen to do, they fill up and fatten human beings' bodies, are praised by them, 518d and will destroy in addition even their original flesh. And they in turn through inexperience will not charge those who feasted them with being responsible for the sicknesses and the loss of their origi- nal flesh; but whoever happen to be in their presence and give some counsel then, when a long time later the former satiety has come to them bringing sickness (since the satiety came about without what is healthy)—these are the ones they will charge, blame, and do some evil, if they are able, whereas they will extol those former ones who 518e were responsible for the evils." And now you, Callicles, are doing something most similar to this: you are extolling human beings who feasted these ones sumptuously on the things they desired. And they say that those men made the city great; but that it is swollen and fes- tering with sores underneath on account of those ancient men, they

519a do not perceive. For without moderation and justice they have filled up the city with harbors, dockyards, walls, tribute, and such drivel; so then when that access of weakness comes, they will charge the counselors then present, but will extol Themistocles, Cimon, and Pericles, the ones responsible for the evils. And perhaps they will attack you, if you don't beware, and my comrade Alcibiades, when they are

519b losing to destruction, in addition to the things they acquired, the original things as well—despite your not being responsible for the evils, though perhaps responsible as accessories.

And indeed there's a thoughtless thing that I now see coming to pass and that I hear about the ancient men. For when the city handles one of the political men as a doer of injustice, I perceive them becoming infuriated and bitterly complaining that they are suffering terrible things; having done many good things for the city, they are in fact being unjustly destroyed by it, as their argument goes. But the

519c whole thing is a lie; for not one leader of a city would ever be unjustly destroyed by that city which he leads. For probably the same thing happens with both those who make themselves out to be political men and those who make themselves out to be sophists. For the sophists, though wise in other respects, do this strange business: for, claiming to be teachers of virtue,[161] they often accuse their students of doing them injustice—depriving them of wages and not giving

519d back other gratitude, though the students have been well treated by them. And what business could be more irrational than this argument, that human beings who have become good and just, have been delivered from injustice by the teacher, and possess justice, do injustice with this that they do not have? Isn't this in your opinion a strange thing, comrade? Truly, Callicles, you compelled me to engage in popular speaking, by not being willing to answer.

CAL.: And you were the one who could not speak, unless someone answered you?

519e SOC.: It would appear so. Now, to be sure, I am drawing my speeches out at length, since you are unwilling to answer me. But, good man, tell me, by the god of Friendship, isn't it irrational in your opinion for one who claims to have made someone good to find fault with him, because, having become and being good through him, he afterwards is base?

161. Gorgias, in contrast, did not make this claim. See note at 457b. But see also 460a–461.

CAL.: In my opinion, at least.

SOC.: So then, do you hear those who claim to educate human beings to virtue saying such things?

520a   CAL.: I do. But what would you say about human beings that are worth nothing?

SOC.: And what would you say about those who, claiming to lead the city and take care that it will be as good as possible, turn around and accuse it of being most base, whenever they happen to? Do you think that these differ in any respect from those? The sophist and the rhetor, you blessed man, are the same thing, or pretty close and nearly resembling, as I was saying to Polus. Through ignorance, however,
520b   you think that the one, rhetoric, is something altogether fine, while you despise the other; but in truth sophistry is as much finer than rhetoric as legislation is finer than the judge's art and gymnastic than medicine. And I for one thought that the popular speakers and sophists were actually the only ones for whom there was no place to find fault with this thing that they themselves educate, on the grounds that it is base toward them; or else by this same argument they must at the same time accuse themselves as well, because they conferred no benefit on those whom they say they benefit. Isn't this the case?
520c   CAL.: Certainly.

SOC.: And in all likelihood, I suppose, for them only is there a place to give away a benefaction without a wage, if what I was saying is true. For someone benefited with another benefaction—for example, becoming swift because of a trainer—might perhaps deprive him of gratitude, if the trainer gave it away to him instead of contracting for a wage and getting the money as nearly as possible at the moment of
520d   giving him a share of swiftness; for it is surely not by slowness, I think, that human beings do injustice, but by injustice, isn't it?

CAL.: Yes.

SOC.: So then if someone takes away this very thing, injustice, he has no fear of ever suffering injustice; but for him alone it is safe to give away this benefaction, if indeed someone is really able to make men good. Isn't it so?

CAL.: I say so.

SOC.: For these reasons therefore, it would appear, it is nothing shameful for a man to take money for giving the other kinds of counsels—such as about building or the other arts.

520e   CAL.: It would appear so, at any rate.

soc.: But certainly about this action—in what way one might be as good as possible and govern his own household or city as well as possible—it is conventionally held to be shameful to refuse to give counsel, unless someone gives one money. Isn't it?

cal.: Yes.

soc.: The cause, clearly, is this: it alone among benefactions makes him who is well treated desire to do good in return, so that it seems to be a fine sign, if the one who does good through this benefaction will be treated well in return; and if not, not.[162] Is that the way it is with these things?

521a cal.: It is.

soc.: Define for me, then, to which manner of caring for the city you are urging me on. Is it that of fighting with the Athenians so that they will be as good as possible, as a doctor would do, or as one who will serve and associate with them with a view to gratification? Tell me the truth, Callicles; for, just as you began being outspoken with me, you are just to end up saying what you think. Now too, speak well and in a nobly born manner.

cal.: Well then, I say as one who will serve.

521b soc.: You are therefore urging me on to engage in flattery, you most nobly born man.

cal.: If it's more pleasant for you to call it Mysian,[163] Socrates. Because if you will not do these things . . .

soc.: Don't say what you have said many times, that whoever wishes will kill me, so that I too will not in turn say that it will be a base man killing a good one; nor that he will confiscate whatever I have, so that I in turn won't say that, having confiscated he won't know how to use them, and just as he confiscated them from me unjustly, so too

521c when he has taken possession he will use them unjustly, and if unjustly, shamefully, and if shamefully, badly.

cal.: How you seem to me, Socrates, to believe you would not suffer one of these things, on the grounds that you dwell out of the way and would not be brought into a law court by a human being who is perhaps altogether degenerate and lowly.

---

162. Protagoras, a rich Sophist, accepted whatever payment a student swore on oath was in his judgment the true value of the teaching he had received.

163. Proverbial words whose meaning, it appears, was something like "to call a spade a spade." A related phrase is "the last of Mysians," (*Theaetetus* 209b) apparently roughly equivalent to "the lowest of the low."

soc.: Then I am truly thoughtless, Callicles, if I don't think that in this city anyone may suffer anything that might happen. This, however, 521d I know well: if I go before a law court about one of these dangers of which you are speaking, some base man will be my prosecutor—for no good[164] person would prosecute a human being who does no injustice—and it would be nothing strange if I should die. Do you wish me to tell you for what reason I expect these things?

cal.: Certainly.

soc.: I think that with a few Athenians—so as not to say myself alone—I put my hand to the true political art and I alone of the men of today practice politics, inasmuch as it is not with a view to gratification that I speak the speeches that I speak on each occasion, but with 521e a view to the best, not to the most pleasant; and since I am unwilling to do what you recommend—"these refined subtleties"—I won't have anything to say in the law court. The same argument applies to me that I was telling Polus: for I will be tried as a doctor accused by a cook would be tried among children. For consider what such a human being, caught in these circumstances, would say in defense, if someone accused him and said, "Boys, this man here has done many bad things to you yourselves; and he corrupts the youngest of you by 522a cutting and burning; and he causes you to be at a loss by reducing and choking you, giving the most bitter draughts and compelling you to be hungry and thirsty—unlike me, who regale you sumptuously with many pleasant things of all sorts." What do you think a doctor, caught up in this bad situation, would have to say? Or if he told the truth, that "I did all these things, boys, in the interest of health," how great a clamor, do you think, would rise up from such judges? Wouldn't it be great?

cal.: Perhaps.

soc.: One must think so, at any rate.[165] Don't you think he would be 522b at a total loss as to what he should say?

cal.: Certainly.

soc.: But I know I too would suffer an experience of this sort if I went before a law court. For I shall not be able to tell them about pleasures that I have furnished them, which they consider benefactions and

---

164. *Chrēstos*, elsewhere translated "useful," has a range of meanings: useful, serviceable, good, worthy, decent, kindly.
165. The manuscripts put these words in Callicles' previous reply; if that is correct, perhaps the "perhaps" should be deleted.

benefits, whereas I envy neither those who supply them nor those to whom they are supplied; and if someone asserts either that I corrupt the younger ones by causing them to be at a loss or that I speak evil of the older ones by making bitter speeches either in private or in pub-

522c lic, I shall not be able to say the truth, that "I say and do all these things justly, gentlemen judges"—to use *your* phrase for them[166]—nor anything else. So that I shall probably suffer whatever may happen.

CAL.: In your opinion, then, Socrates, is a human being in a fine state, when he's in such a condition in the city, powerless to help himself?

SOC.: If, at any rate, he has that one thing, Callicles, which you have agreed on many times—if he has helped himself so as neither to have

522d said nor to have done anything unjust as regards either human beings or gods. For this kind of helping oneself has been agreed on by us many times to be the strongest. If someone convicted me by refutation of being powerless to help myself or another with this kind of help, then I would be ashamed, whether refuted among many, among few, or alone by one man only, and if I should die because of this incapacity, I would be sorely vexed; but if I came to my end through lack of flattering rhetoric, I know well that you would see me bear-

522e ing death easily. For no one fears dying itself, who is not all in all most irrational and unmanly, but he fears doing injustice; for to arrive in Hades with one's soul full of many unjust deeds is the ultimate of all evils. And if you wish, I am willing to tell you a rational account, that this is so.

CAL.: Well, since you have finished the other things, finish this too.

523a SOC.: Hear then, as they say, a very fine rational account, which you consider a myth, as I think, but I consider it a rational account; for I shall tell you the things I am going to tell as being true. For just as Homer says, Zeus, Poseidon, and Pluto divided the rule among themselves, after they took it over from their father.[167] Now in the time of Cronos there was the following law concerning human be-

166. In the *Apology*, Socrates addresses the large jury as "Athenian men"; as one might expect from this passage of the *Gorgias*, he uses "gentlemen judges" (more literally, "men judges") only to address the minority who voted for his acquittal (*Apology* 40a).

167. In the *Iliad*, 15.187–93, Poseidon, in anger at Zeus's command that he leave the fighting at Troy, refers to this division to justify his own title to equal standing with Zeus. Homer there uses the name Hades rather than Pluto. The term "take over" suggests ordinary inheritance. Socrates is silent here on the tale of violence against their father, Cronos, as told by Hesiod (*Theogony* 453–506 and 617 ff.), which he criticizes in the *Republic* 377e–378e and the *Euthyphro* 5e–6b.

ings, and it exists always and still to this day among the gods, that he
523b among human beings who went through life justly and piously,
when he came to his end, would go away to the islands of the blessed
to dwell in total happiness apart from evils, while he who lived unjustly and godlessly would go to the prison of retribution and judgment, which they call Tartarus. In the time of Cronos and while Zeus's
possession of rule was still new, the judges of these living men were
themselves living, and passed judgment on that day on which the
men were going to come to their end; and so the judgments were decided badly. So then Pluto and those in charge from the islands of the
523c blessed went and said to Zeus that unworthy human beings were fre-
quenting them in both places. So Zeus said, "Nay, I," he said, "shall
stop this from coming to pass. For now the judgments are judged
badly. For those on trial," he said, "are tried clothed; for they are tried
living. Hence many," he said, "who have base souls are clothed in
fine bodies, ancestry, and wealth, and when the trial takes place,
many witnesses go with them to bear witness that they have lived
523d justly; the judges, then, are driven out of their senses by these men,
and at the same time they themselves pass judgment clothed as well,
with eyes and ears and the whole body, like a screen, covering over
their soul. All these things come in their way—both their own clothes
and those of the men being tried. First, therefore," he said, "one must
stop them from foreknowing their death, for now they foreknow it.
523e Prometheus[168] has therefore already been told to stop this in them.
Next, one must try them naked, without all these things; for they
must be tried when they are dead. And he who decides the trial must
be naked, dead, and must with his soul itself contemplate the soul itself of each man immediately upon his death, bereft of all kinsfolk
and having left all that adornment[169] behind on earth, so that the trial
may be just. Knowing these things before you, I have therefore made
524a my sons judges—two from Asia, Minos and Rhadamanthus, and one
from Europe, Aeacus; so then, when they have come to their end,
these ones will pass judgment in the meadow, at the fork in the road
from which two roads lead, one to the islands of the blessed, the

168. In *Prometheus Bound* by Aeschylus, Prometheus, a master of devices, reports that he
stopped mortals from foreseeing their doom by causing blind hopes to dwell within
them, but these deeds along with his giving men fire and all arts were done against Zeus's
will.
169. *Kosmos*.

other to Tartarus.[170] Rhadamanthus will try those from Asia, and Aeacus those from Europe; to Minos I shall give, as the privilege of age, to pass further judgment, when the other two are at a loss about something, so that the decision about the journey for human beings may be as just as possible.

524b   These are the things, Callicles, that I have heard and believe to be true; and from these speeches I calculate that something of this sort follows. Death, as it seems to me, happens to be nothing other than the separation of two things, the soul and the body, from each other. When, therefore, they are separated from each other, each of them is in a condition not much worse than when the human being was alive, and the body has its own nature, the cares taken of it, and its 524c   sufferings all manifest. For example, if the body of someone still living was big either by nature or rearing or both, this man's corpse will be big too when he is dead, and if stout, stout too when he is dead, and thus with regard to other things; and if, again, he made a practice of letting his hair grow long, this man's corpse too will be long-haired. Again, if someone while alive was a rascal in need of a whipping and had the traces of blows—scars[171]—on his body, either from whips or other wounds, one can see that his body, when he has died, has these things. Or if someone's limbs were broken or distorted 524d   while he was alive, these same things will be manifest when he has died. In one speech: of such a sort as he prepared himself to be in regard to his body while he lived, all these things or many of them will be manifest for some time also when he has come to his end. Now this same thing, then, seems to me to hold for the soul as well, Callicles: all things are manifest in the soul, when it has been stripped naked of the body—both the things of nature and the sufferings that the human being had in his soul through the pursuit of each kind of business. So when they have arrived before the judge, those from 524e   Asia before Rhadamanthus, Rhadamanthus halts them and contemplates each one's soul, not knowing whose it is; but often, laying hold of the great king or some other king or potentate, he perceives that there is nothing healthy in the soul, but it has been severely whipped 525a   and is filled with scars from false oaths and injustice, which each ac-

---

170. The island of Crete, from which Minos and Rhadamanthus come, is counted as belonging to Asia. The word translated "fork in the road" is more literally "triple road."
171. The word translated "scar" in this passage, *oulē*, is part of the word *hupoulos*, translated "festering with sores underneath" at 518e and 480b.

tion of his stamped upon his soul, and all things are crooked from lying and boasting, and there is nothing straight on account of his having been reared without truth; and he sees the soul full of asymme-
try and ugliness from arrogant power, luxury, wanton insolence,[172]
and incontinence of actions; and having seen it he sends it away dishonorably, straight to the prison, having come to which it is going to
endure fitting sufferings.

525b   It is fitting for everyone who is subject to retribution and is correctly visited with retribution by another either to become better and
be profited or to become an example to others, so that others, seeing
him suffer whatever he suffers, may be afraid and become better.
And some there are who are benefited and pay the just penalty, by
gods and human beings—those who err in making curable errors;
nevertheless the benefit comes about for them through pains and
griefs both here and in Hades, for it is not possible otherwise that
525c   they be released from injustice. On the other hand, the examples
come into being from those who have done the ultimate injustices
and have become incurable[173] through such unjust deeds; and these
men are no longer profited themselves, inasmuch as they are incurable, but others are profited who see these men suffering on account
of their errors the greatest, most painful, and most fearful sufferings
for all time, simply hung up there in the prison in Hades as examples—spectacles and admonitions to those of the unjust who are for-
525d   ever arriving. I assert that Archelaus too will be one of these, if what
Polus says is true, and whoever else is a tyrant of this sort. And I think
that the majority of these examples, indeed, have come into being
from tyrants, kings, potentates, and those who engage in the affairs
of the cities; for these through having a free hand[174] make the greatest and most impious errors. And Homer too bears witness to these
things, for he has represented those who pay retribution for all time
525e   in Hades as kings and potentates—Tantalus, Sisyphus, and Tityus;
but no one has represented Thersites,[175] or anyone else who was a

---

172. *Hubris:* see *Phaedrus* 238a.

173. Dodds provides a valuable observation: "incurables" occur also in the myths of the *Republic* and *Phaedo*, but in the *Phaedrus* myth all souls regain their wings eventually, and no eternal punishment is threatened in the *Laws*.

174. *Exousia* can mean power, authority, abuse of power, arrogance, magistracy or office, freedom. It was translated "arrogant power" at 525a, "freedom" at 461e.

175. Tantalus, Sisyphus, and Tityus are observed by Odysseus in *Odyssey* 11.576–600. Thersites, described as the ugliest man in the Greek expedition against Troy, spoke abusively

base private man, as held fast by great retributions on the grounds of being incurable (for I don't think he had a free hand to do so, and accordingly he was happier than those who did); for indeed, Callicles,

526a those human beings who become exceedingly base are also from among the powerful. Nothing, to be sure, prevents good men from coming into being even among these, and those who become such are exceedingly worthy of admiration; for it is difficult, Callicles, and worthy of much praise, that one who has come to have a very free hand to do injustice should pass through life justly. But a few such do come into being, seeing that both here and elsewhere men have come into being—and I think there will be in the future—who are noble

526b and good with respect to this virtue of justly managing whatever someone entrusts to them; one even became altogether well spoken of among the other Greeks as well, Aristides the son of Lysimachus;[176] but the majority of potentates, you best of men, become bad. So then as I was saying, when Rhadamanthus gets hold of some such man, he does not know anything else about him—neither who he is nor from whom he is descended—but only that he is someone base; and having perceived this, he sends him away to Tartarus, putting a mark on him indicating whether he seems to be curable or incurable;

526c and when he has arrived there, he suffers fitting things. Sometimes, beholding another soul that has lived piously and with truth—a private man's or someone else's, but mostly, as I for one assert, Callicles, a philosopher's who has done his own business and not been a busybody in life[177]—Rhadamanthus admires it and sends it away to the islands of the blessed. And Aeacus too does these same things; each of them judges holding a staff. And Minos sits overseeing them, he

526d alone holding the golden scepter, as Homer's Odysseus says he saw him, "holding the golden scepter, dispensing right[178] to the dead."

So then I, Callicles, have been persuaded by these speeches, and I

---

against the leaders; Odysseus, admitting that Thersites is a clear-voiced public speaker (*agorētēs*), rebuked him and beat him with the scepter, to the general approbation of the Greek host (*Iliad* 2.211–77).

176. Aristides, usually further designated "the Just." See notes at 503c, 516d, and 517a.

177. One is reminded of the definition of justice stated in book 4 of the *Republic:* doing one's own things and not being a busybody (433a). *Polupragmosunē,* "being a busybody" or more literally "being busy with much," is perhaps on the way to *panourgia,* "doing everything" (see note at *Gorgias* 499b).

178. Or "giving judgments": *themisteuon,* derived from *themis* (right, judgment, law); see second note at 497c. The quotation is from *Odyssey* 11.569.

consider how I might show as healthy a soul as possible to him who decides the trial. Bidding farewell, then, to the honors that come from the many human beings, I shall try both to live and to die, when I die,

526e practicing the truth and really being as good as I have power to be. And I urge on all other human beings as well, to the extent of my power—and to be sure I also urge you on in return[179]—toward this life and this contest, which I assert is the one, instead of all the contests here; and I reproach you that you will not be able to help yourself, when you have the judgment and the trial of which I was speak-

527a ing just now; but when you have come to that judge, the son of Aegina,[180] and when that one seizes hold of you and brings you in, you will be gaping and dizzy there no less than I here, and perhaps someone will dishonorably strike you a crack on the jaw and completely trample you in the mud.

Now then, perhaps these things seem to you to be told as a myth, like an old wives' tale, and you despise them; and it would be not at all amazing to despise them, if we were able to seek somewhere and find better and truer things than they. Now, however, you see that, though you are three, and are the wisest of the Greeks of today—you,

527b Polus, and Gorgias—you are not able to prove that one should live any other life than this one, which is manifestly advantageous in that place too. But among so many speeches, the others are refuted and this speech alone remains fixed: that one must beware of doing injustice more than of suffering injustice, and more than everything, a man must take care not to seem to be good but to be so, both in private and in public; and if someone becomes bad in some respect, he must be punished, and this is the second good after being just—be-

527c coming so and paying the just penalty by being punished; and one must flee from all flattery, concerning both oneself and others, and concerning both few men and many; and one must use rhetoric thus, always aiming at what is just, and so for every other action.

Be persuaded, then, and follow me there where, having arrived, you will be happy both living and when you have come to your end, as the argument indicates. And let someone despise you as foolish and trample you in the mud, if he wishes—and yes, by Zeus, confi-

527d dently let him knock you this dishonorable blow; for you will suffer

179. That is, in response to Callicles' different urging on of him.
180. The nymph Aegina bore Aeacus to Zeus.

nothing terrible, if you really are noble and good, practicing virtue. And after we have practiced in common thus, then at last, if it seems we ought, shall we apply ourselves to political affairs; or we shall take counsel on what sort of thing seems good to us then, when we are better at taking counsel than now. For it is shameful to be in the condition that we now appear to be in, and then to behave like youths as if we were something, when things never seem the same 527e to us as regards the same things—and this as regards the greatest things. To such a degree of lack of education have we come! Let us then use the argument that has now revealed itself like a leader, which indicates to us that this way of life is best: to live and to die practicing both justice and the rest of virtue. Let us then follow this argument, and let us urge the others on to it, not to that one which you believe in and to which you urge me on; for it is worth nothing, Callicles.

The Rhetoric of Justice in Plato's *Gorgias*

Socrates wants to talk to Gorgias. In contrast with the *Republic*, where Pole-marchus must playfully compel Socrates to join the group whose leisurely discussion will investigate justice, the discussion here arises from Socrates' own initiative. There is something definite that he wants to talk about with Gorgias, and he blames his late arrival on his companion Chaerephon. By arriving late, they miss the display speeches for which Gorgias is best known and instead engage in Socrates' characteristic activity, conversation or dialectic, directed toward finding out what Socrates wants to know: what it is that Gorgias professes and what the power of his art is.

One can hardly doubt that Socrates already knew Gorgias to be a rheto-rician. Furthermore, it becomes altogether clear early in Socrates' discussion with Polus that Socrates has quite a fully developed conception of what something called rhetoric is, which he takes to be not a true art but a kind of merely empirically developed flattery. Socrates nonetheless wants something from Gorgias, perhaps the most famous practitioner and teacher of rhetoric: that something appears at first to be a more precise under-standing of rhetoric and its power according to Gorgias; eventually Socra-tes seems to wish to involve Gorgias in some joint endeavor, whose first product is Gorgias's successfully urging Callicles to complete the discus-sion with Socrates.

A first element of Socrates' preexisting view of rhetoric speedily comes to light in his rejection of Polus's speech about Gorgias's art. Polus, Socra-tes says, has praised Gorgias's art as if it were being attacked rather than saying what it is. According to Socrates, whereas dialectic seeks to state *what* a thing is, rhetoric praises or blames by proclaiming *what kind* of thing something is. At first sight rhetoric involves praise and blame, whereas dialectic seeks knowledge that is more fundamental and, perhaps, dispassionate.

Chaerephon takes Socrates' place, at Socrates' direction, to begin the inquiry into Gorgias's activity. Perhaps responding to this situation as somehow disrespectful of Gorgias, Polus intervenes to answer in his place, on the grounds that Gorgias is probably tired from all he has already presented. In this first round of discussion, Gorgias's student seems to leave Chaerephon nonplussed, so that Socrates himself must intervene. Polus's own shortcomings do not emerge until later. In any case, this early discussion prompts us to reflect on the relation of teachers and students, and especially on the degree of success a teacher may have in passing on what he may know.

Socrates cleverly sets up his own conversation with Gorgias so as strongly to encourage, if not absolutely to require, short answers. The brevity of the answers about what rhetoric is causes the first definitions to be too broad or universal or inclusive; the definition is narrowed down through Socrates' questioning and, in that sense, under his guidance. Socrates takes the direction of focusing in on the subject matter of the speeches with which rhetoric is concerned. The first clear mention of political subject matter (apart from Callicles' initial reference to battle) arises tangentially in Socrates' comparison of his own use of language in asking several sequential questions with a formula used by drafters of proposals for the assembly of the people.

Gorgias's first statements present his art of rhetoric as universal in two ways. First, Gorgias asserts that, a rhetor himself, he can make other men rhetors, both in Athens and elsewhere. Second, his first brief definitions seem to give rhetoric a universal scope, as *the* art that deals with speeches. Socrates' line of questioning toward the subject matter of rhetoric's speeches leads Gorgias to abandon the possibility of presenting rhetoric as a universal art of speech or persuasiveness in all cases whatsoever, in favor of defining rhetoric as an art that persuades political gatherings about political matters, above all justice. Gorgias has given many an exhibition, wherein his practice is to open himself up to questions, and he confidently notes that he has not been asked a new question for many years. Surely someone of his eminence and experience has thought over the alternative not taken. Further on in the discussion he distinguishes between the capacity of rhetoric and the political goals it enables one to attain (when he claims at 452d to be a craftsman of "the greatest good and the cause both of freedom for human beings . . . and of rule over others"). Why, then, does Gorgias go along with the political direction taken by Socrates rather than try to maintain a conception of rhetoric as the universal and comprehensive art of speeches? The most likely explanation concerns Gorgias's self-interest as a teacher: Socrates' line of questioning highlights the practical application of Gorgias's art in the areas in which most students want to use it: politics in general and judicial proceedings in particular. Gorgias cheerfully follows Socrates' lead because Socrates helps out his affairs, as Socrates explicitly notes a bit later (455c).

It is doubtless Gorgias's desire to attract students that leads him to make or nearly to make (because he leaves in a hedging word or two) certain overstatements about the power of his art. In response to Socrates' observations that people contest what the greatest human good is, the doctor claiming that it is health, the trainer that it is strength and beauty, the businessman that it is wealth, Gorgias claims that through rhetoric one may have the doctor or trainer as one's slave and that the businessman will turn out to be making money for you the rhetor and not for himself. At this point, Gorgias shows no concern about whether such use of the power of persuasion is in accordance with justice.

Socrates draws Gorgias out further by expressing bafflement at just how and where the rhetor would exert the power of persuasion, given that for so many objects of deliberation we have known experts whom it would seem reasonable chiefly to consult. Gorgias claims that rhetoric shows its power precisely in the area of public deliberation. In fact not the several experts but the skilled rhetors prevail in public discussions. Rhetoric is so very powerful that its practitioners prevail over all others, including those with superior knowledge in the area under deliberation; it holds all powers "so to speak" under itself. Gorgias can persuade patients to submit to medical treatment when doctors, including his brother, fail to persuade. Although that example is not explicitly discussed in the rest of the dialogue, it is crucial for understanding the character and potential of rhetoric; rhetoric need not always be mere flattery directed to base ends; it can assist the true expert in attaining the practical goal at which he aims but which he cannot attain by the means of his art alone. In other words, rhetoric as practiced by Gorgias can provide indispensable service to a true art.

The rhetor, Gorgias claims, could defeat the doctor in any political contest, even in the election of a city's public health officer. Having stated this bold claim, Gorgias prudently reins himself in, aware that such a use of rhetoric's power seems unjust abuse from the standpoint of the public good or the just claims of competent experts. If rhetors were seen as using rhetoric's great power unjustly, would not political communities then rightly decide to ban rhetoric and to exile teachers of rhetoric like Gorgias? In response to this possibility, Gorgias immediately transforms his speech, as if rhetoric had been charged with injustice, into a defense of rhetoric and its teachers. Like any other competitive capacity, Gorgias argues, rhetoric is meant to be put to just use. If someone misuses it, that one and not the teacher of rhetoric is guilty of injustice and deserving of blame and punishment.

Socrates refutes Gorgias by bringing to light a contradiction. On the one hand Gorgias has been drawn out by Socrates to assert both that rhetoric is concerned with speeches about justice and injustice and that Gorgias teaches students justice if they do not already know it. On the other, Gorgias expresses awareness that some students of rhetoric may put the art to unjust use. It is striking that development of those assertions into a clear contradiction depends on some questionable claims, such as that learning what justice is makes one just (and hence a doer of just deeds) in the same way that learning music makes one musical. Why does a skilled speaker like Gorgias not attack the weak links in Socrates' argument? I believe that Gorgias chooses the lesser evil of silence over further argument because he realizes that he has fallen into an uncomfortable and dangerous area of discussion. He has claimed to be nearly all-powerful at persuasion and has been compelled to admit that his students either know justice or learn it from him. If students act unjustly, then either Gorgias does not really concern himself with their knowledge of justice (and is thus clearly irresponsible in giving them the power of rhetoric) or else his own ability to persuade them (of the goodness of justice, for instance) is not efficacious. In fact Gorgias *is* worried about rhetoric's unseemly reputation in the matter of justice.

This brief dialogue between Socrates and Gorgias points toward, without explicitly stating, other tensions in Gorgias's position. On the one hand, he is an intellectual, whose art as a product of human intelligence is universal or cosmopolitan. Thus, he claims that he can make people into rhetors anywhere, in Athens or wherever, and he claims for rhetoric a universal power of enabling human beings to provide freedom for themselves. But on the other hand, the most widely desired application of Gorgias's art is political, and in this respect an irreducible particularity of politics asserts itself against rhetoric's would-be universality: thus Gorgias claims that rhetoric can provide rule over others only in each man's own city. The universal knowledge or art of rhetoric can be universally applied to secure freedom for each individual, but for the goal of political rule, the art's effective application is limited to the particular citizen's own community.

A parallel tension in Gorgias comes to sight from reflection on the twofold character of persuasion that he elaborates in response to Socrates' questioning. Rhetoric as it has emerged in the discussion persuades political gatherings, but such persuasion is not the only kind. Gorgias is a teacher of rhetoric, and he believes that his teaching too is a form of persuasion—a form that conveys knowledge, which can only mean true knowledge, to students. Gorgias's emphatic agreement, highlighted with a superlative, that "they [teachers] persuade most of all," suggests that in one way he values his universal knowledge most highly. Nonetheless, political/rhetorical persuasion, of the sort chiefly brought to light in Socrates' and Gorgias's discussion, produces mere persuasion without knowledge, and it is chiefly for this that most students come to him to learn. They care not about knowledge (let alone justice) but about how to produce the nondidactic mere persuasion that is useful for political purposes.

Another complex tension in Gorgias's position or way of life involves private concerns and public purposes. Gorgias himself does not focus his life on public goals. His action in a public capacity as ambassador of his native city of Leontini seems to have been the exception in a generally private life, a life spent mainly in a cosmopolitan manner as he moved from city to city teaching his art. Gorgias worries about rhetoric's reputation for encouraging injustice, as we have seen, and speaks defensively on that issue. And yet he also appeals, though with some discretion, to unjust gains that potential students might possibly make: when he claims that the rhetor can cause the businessman to make money for the rhetor rather than for himself, Gorgias evokes the factions between rich and poor and the consequent confiscations and exilings that caused such turmoil in the Greek cities. Counting on his rhetoric to provide himself with freedom (and wealth), Gorgias appears not to take seriously the most important public concern, the concern for justice. He knows that a visible or prominent pursuit like rhetorical instruction and practice cannot profess indifference, let alone hostility, to justice, but his own most serious concerns lie elsewhere. Some of his students must surely wish to use rhetoric chiefly for political advancement, but Gorgias himself seems to pursue private advantage, reputation, intellectual activity, and freedom. Precisely how rhetoric is to be used in the public arena becomes a theme explored in Socrates' discussions with Polus and Callicles.

It is often said that Plato in the *Gorgias* treats Gorgias unfairly and nastily while attacking rhetoric harshly. I believe that this impression, though understandable on the basis of Socrates' decidedly confrontational tone in the later arguments with Polus and Callicles, is mistaken as regards his discussion with Gorgias. In fact, however, Socrates treats Gorgias with delicacy and tact, verging on apparent respect. He takes great care to explain that he is not attacking Gorgias, nor is he making trouble for personal reasons but only for the sake of pursuing the argument clearly. Most important, Socrates states no harsh conclusions about Gorgias's stance toward justice. For example, although bringing out that Gorgias's rhetoric about justice is of the kind that merely persuades the many without teaching genuine knowledge, Socrates does not point out that a judicial rhetor may often wish to obscure or confound the issues of justice for the sake of winning the case. With no reference to such a speaker's likely desire to obfuscate or distort the truth in a judicial case, Socrates gives instead a remarkably exculpatory reason why Gorgias's judicial rhetoric is merely persuasive: "For [a rhetor] would not be able, I suppose, to teach so large a mob such great matters in a short time" (455a).

Socrates does bring to light some contradiction in Gorgias's position, but not in a harsh or condemnatory way. He refrains from explicitly drawing the likely inference that Gorgias devotes little effort to promoting the just use of his teaching and discouraging the unjust. Rather, Socrates merely observes that a contradiction exists between Gorgias's assertion that he does teach students about justice and his awareness that some students may put rhetoric to unjust use, and explicitly concludes only that the full elaboration of exactly what Gorgias's rhetoric is would require much more discussion. Socrates confronts Gorgias with unpalatable alternatives: either to admit to little or no care about the justice of his students; or to confess that his rhetoric is decidedly limited in its power, as exemplified by his inability to persuade students to be concerned with justice; or, as is most likely the case, both. In this situation Gorgias falls prudently silent, perhaps feeling a puzzled gratitude as to why Socrates did not proceed to drive the problem home more starkly.

Perhaps too Gorgias is intrigued by the paradoxical vision of rhetoric called forth by Socrates' argument, namely a rhetoric that could only be used justly. Gorgias, after all, appears to be by and large a contented person, famous, wealthy, and respected. He even seems reasonably satisfied with the state of his knowledge, to judge from the air of complacency conveyed by his claim not to have heard a new question in many years. The only fly in the ointment of his full satisfaction is the questionable reputation of rhetoric in some quarters because of its dubious relation to justice. The curious argument by which Socrates refutes Gorgias also suggests a possible art of rhetoric dealing with justice that would of necessity be available only for just use. Although it seems no slander to guess that Gorgias is not deeply concerned with justice for its own sake, Socrates' suggestion might interest him precisely as removing the one remaining problem that mars full contentment in his activity. This purpose could be the basis of an alliance between Socrates and Gorgias who, though competitors, have engaged in no hostile acts. This possibility of a just rhetoric is central to Socrates' discussions with Polus and Callicles in the rest of the dialogue.

We may perhaps conclude that Socrates has learned from Gorgias what he originally sought to know, namely the character and power of Gorgias's art. It does not seem, however, that Socrates learns anything much more from Gorgias in the arguments that follow. What, then, is Socrates' purpose hereafter? Let us simply note that what Socrates in fact accomplishes is somehow to engage Gorgias in these discussions. When Polus fails to ask questions that clarify the meaning of Socrates' own definition of rhetoric, Gorgias intervenes to resolve the perplexity and learn what Socrates means. And again, when Callicles would prefer to give up the discussion in irritation, Gorgias intervenes to keep it going and bring it to completion.

Polus rejects the idea that Socrates has uncovered any real contradiction in Gorgias's account of rhetoric and angrily accuses Socrates of rudeness (or rusticity) for leading people on and tripping them up. He attributes Gorgias's difficulty in the argument to his sense of shame, which led Gorgias to concede that he teaches students to know the just, noble, and good things if they do not know them already. In other words, Polus implicitly chooses one of the alternatives neither of which Gorgias explicitly accepted. In order to maintain that rhetoric and rhetors have great power, Polus is willing tacitly to admit that Gorgias probably does not in fact devote much effort to teaching justice to his students or persuading them to be just.

Polus attributes Gorgias's concession to shame. Gorgias has indeed explicitly stated that he was motivated by shame at one point in the discussion: after Gorgias's longest speech extolling the power of rhetoric and then defending it against the charge of injustice, Socrates indicated that he would wish to continue the conversation if Gorgias like him wanted to pursue the truth; Gorgias said he was willing (for who, after all, could wish to proclaim indifference to the truth?) but that others might wish to be doing something else; when the others expressed eagerness to hear more, Gorgias stated that it would be shameful for him not to be willing to continue, because he himself had invited people to ask whatever anyone wished (458d–e). Gorgias's shame would derive, it seems, from being observed to violate an explicit agreement. I doubt, however, that the concession mentioned by Polus comes from shame; as I have already suggested, it seems more reasonable to view Gorgias's concession as motivated by prudent caution regarding rhetoric's need for a defense in regard to justice.

Polus himself appears to have more of a sense of shame, in fact, than Gorgias: he is angry at Socrates' having tripped up Gorgias and displays great eagerness to get Socrates to admit that rhetoric's power is something fine; and his ultimately being refuted by Socrates stems from his admitting that doing injustice is something more shameful than suffering it. However that may be, Polus surely lacks the caution and prudence of his teacher. Soon he rashly asserts that rhetoric helps one to accomplish powerful deeds without regard to their justice or injustice, and he even goes so far as to speak of rhetors and unjust tyrants as comparable in power and happiness. In provoking these statements from Polus, Socrates displays before Gorgias's own eyes the shortcomings and dangers that come from Gorgias's inadequate attention to teaching justice. Gorgias's student openly praises the works of injustice, leaving himself and rhetoric vulnerable to the city's accusation of injustice. Furthermore, in pursuing his line of argument, Polus speaks of a tyrant, Archelaus of Macedon, as a great example of successful injustice. But as we can see from Polus's own account of Archelaus's deeds, such a tyrant does not found his power chiefly on rhetoric. Hence the limits on rhetoric's power in politics, contrary to the intended thrust of Gorgias's claims, become starkly visible.

While engaged in harsh refutation of Polus, Socrates continues his kidglove treatment of Gorgias himself. Most notable in this regard is Socrates' expressed reluctance to present his own characterization of rhetoric, for fear that Gorgias might think him to be satirizing Gorgias's activity. He points out, moreover, that what he says might well not apply to Gorgias's art, in that we have not seen precisely what Gorgias's rhetoric is. Socrates presents his long account of rhetoric as a part of flattery only when permitted, indeed urged, to do so by Gorgias.

Socrates' own discourse on rhetoric as a kind of flattery narrows rhetoric's scope to the domain of justice (setting aside its broader deliberative uses, noted by Gorgias earlier—to become public health officer, for instance, or to propose and carry measures for military fortifications). Per-

haps the reason for this narrowing is that Socrates is using the issue of justice in his effort to engage Gorgias's attention. Perhaps it is also that the
combative and angry Polus takes deeds like confiscating property, exiling,
and putting to death to be the most impressive displays of power—actions
properly used as typical judicial punishments (but whose actual justice
Polus unlike Socrates considers irrelevant to their worth as signs of power).
Socrates thus depicts rhetoric here not only as not an art but also as far less
comprehensive or exalted in its domain than politics: the art of politics
contains both the higher and more comprehensive art of legislation and
the remedial art of justice (taken chiefly as just punishing); rhetoric is a flattering imitation only of justice.

Polus angrily defends a view about justice, intellectually rooted in sophistic teachings, according to which unjust deeds typically benefit the
doer, provided one can avoid paying the just penalty, which penalty is
believed to be a bad thing for the doer. Socrates calls Polus's view widely
shared, or shared by everyone but himself: the point here is not that what
Polus says is the official conventional view, but that most of us do in fact
hold unjust gains to be good, feel anger at the unjust advantage achieved
by the unjust, and wish angrily to inflict harms on them in retaliation.
Polus's anger at the apparent prosperity of the unjust turns back on the
conventional view of justice itself in the mode of a cynical debunking
(which surely is no less widespread and may even prevail among intellectuals today). In refuting Polus, Socrates seeks with apparent success to turn
Polus's energy, anger, and taste for violent deeds toward support for the
city's punitive justice. Under Socrates' direction, justice turns out to be
medical treatment for sick souls. Socrates is in no position to heal Polus by
punishing him for his unjust opinions with the sorts of spectacular deeds
that Polus admires; but Socrates does present his own just argument as
the medicine that Polus needs. As Gorgias can make the treatments of his
brother the doctor effective by persuading the patients to undergo them,
so Socrates steers Polus toward accusing those who are unjust—even or
especially friends, family, and himself—so that they can be made better
through just punishments. The one extensive speech by Polus against
which Socrates raises no objection is his account of the deeds of Archelaus,
meant to show their injustice and Archelaus's character as a tyrant—a prosecutor's speech of accusation overlaid with the cynical intellectual's bitter
revelation of the rewards for injustice.

The discussion between Socrates and Polus contains several moments
wherein Socrates contrasts his way of refuting or persuading an inter-

locutor to various approaches to persuasion taken by Polus. At the beginning of this discussion Socrates once again seeks to ban long speeches, which he had earlier called characteristic of rhetoric rather than dialectic or conversation. After his own lengthy discourse on rhetoric, however, he rejects Polus's approaches for reasons other than length.

On one occasion he blames Polus for calling witnesses, like a forensic rhetor: Socrates rejects such procedures as incapable of attaining truth, for one person might be right against the contrary testimony of many witnesses. Socrates goes so far as to suggest that everyone, everywhere on the political spectrum of Athens, would tend to agree with Polus rather than with him, but asserts that such political modes of deciding questions fall short of truth. His own approach is to compel the one person with whom he is conversing to agree with him, and he claims that this establishes truth more reliably than many witnesses. Whereas Polus's manner of arguing is political or judicial, Socrates' is that of one man alone, a private man who does not even converse with the many. On another occasion, when Polus vividly evokes the pain and distress suffered by the doer of injustice who is being punished, Socrates rejects Polus's approach as mere scare tactics, unworthy of serious rational consideration. Yet again, Socrates dismisses Polus for simply trying to laugh an argument down, rather than providing serious argument. Socrates is clearly not moved by Polus's means of persuasion. One must wonder to what extent Socrates himself truly persuades Polus. Polus does appear to be compelled and as such impressed by Socrates' arguments. It soon becomes clear, however, that Callicles is not.

The position that Socrates compels Polus to accept is, as Socrates explicitly notes, opposed to most people's views. (Socrates surely exaggerates the opposition, in that an aspect, at least, of most people's views is indeed that doing unjust deeds is shameful and thus in some sense bad.) Especially contrary to ordinary opinion is the consequence that we should use rhetoric to accuse our family, our friends, and ourselves of injustice in order to be justly punished and so made better in our souls—and Socrates even briefly alludes to defending and by inference to accusing one's fatherland, as though some worldwide court could judge and inflict just punishment. But as if this were not paradoxical enough, Socrates proceeds still deeper into paradox—whether to demonstrate the full extent of his mastery in argument over Polus or to provoke the vehement objection of Callicles—by positing two dubious premises in order to draw a still more outrageous conclusion: If one should ever do evil to someone, such as an enemy (a premise that Socrates elsewhere denies, most notably in his discussion about justice with Polemarchus in the first book of the *Republic*); and if one might encourage and facilitate another person's doing of injustice while successfully avoiding harm to oneself (which is on its face so highly unlikely that Socrates uses its unlikeliness in his *Apology* as a way of proving to Meletus that he would not corrupt anyone voluntarily); then one should try to preserve one's enemy eternally, or as long as possible, in his doing injustice, so that he may suffer the greatest possible ills of the soul.

Though Polus had earlier protested vehemently against Socrates' maintaining strange positions, by now this young intellectual appears to have been bewitched or attracted by the Socratic extreme of paradox. Not so Callicles, a young man of political ambition. He finds Socrates' arguments so contrary to common sense that he asks Chaerephon whether Socrates might not be joking. Assured by Chaerephon that Socrates seems extraordinarily serious, Callicles asks Socrates himself about the issue, noting that if he is serious, we all act just opposite to how we should.

The rather long answer that Socrates gives to Callicles' question aims, first, at making Socrates' strange statements somehow comprehensible to Callicles, by showing what experiences Socrates and Callicles have in common. They are both lovers, each passionately drawn to a young man, either Alcibiades or Dēmos, and to something else, either philosophy or the Athenian people (*dēmos*), respectively. Socrates speaks of his own loves in a manner that suggests the predominance of love of wisdom (the relationship, indeed harmony, of philosophy and pederasty are depicted by Socrates in the *Phaedrus*); how the two loves of Callicles relate to each other, apart from the accident of their being homonyms, remains unclear. This theme of *erōs* comes from out of the blue—it seems wholly absent from Socrates' discussions with Gorgias and Polus—and its introduction by Socrates must, I think, be understood as based on his knowledge or divination of Callicles' erotic character, to which he somehow appeals so as to try to make himself intelligible to Callicles. Love is so powerful that it can motivate speeches that are bizarre indeed, in their aim to please the beloved.

Secondly, however, Socrates thus formulates the basic difference between himself and Callicles. Socrates' beloved philosophy displays constancy, whereas Callicles' beloved *dēmos* is changeable and capricious. In Callicles' reaction to Socrates' speech, difference predominates over shared experience (surely in part because of the rather demeaning picture Socrates paints of Callicles' constantly changing his stated positions at the fickle people's bidding) to such a degree as to constitute or provoke fundamental opposition. Callicles accordingly chooses to respond with an attack on

Socrates and on philosophy. Socrates, Callicles says, is a tricky arguer, who trips people up by stealthily switching the basis of discussion from nature to law or convention, or vice versa, in order to produce contradiction. In the previous discussion with Polus, according to Callicles' analysis, Socrates managed to refute Polus's judgment that suffering injustice is worse than doing it (which is true from the standpoint of nature) on the basis of Polus's concession that doing injustice is more shameful than suffering injustice (which is true according to conventional opinion). Callicles' calling Socrates a "popular speaker"—despite Callicles's recognition that if Socrates' opinions were true we all should have to try to live quite otherwise than we do—presumably means to unveil and denounce Socrates' reliance on conventional moral opinions. In Callicles' view, however, nature and convention are mostly opposed, and the standpoint of nature is preferable. Conventional justice, which praises equality and decries taking more than an equal share, is a conspiracy of the mediocre and weak against the strong and potentially great. Callicles describes how the opinion of the majority tries to bewitch and enslave the better sort (not unlike Socrates' description in the *Republic* of public education by the many as so strong that any private education is hard put to hold out against it). Indeed, for Callicles, conventional justice does injustice (from the higher standpoint of nature) to the superior types. Callicles does not simply criticize and reject justice (as perhaps Gorgias does, or Thrasymachus in the *Republic*) and then proceed to calculate his own best interests; he vividly states his belief that nature displays a higher and truer justice, in accordance with which the strong should rule the weak and take more. In other words, Callicles sees nature as a ground of moral order. It is not merely that conventional justice is illusory and deceptive, so that the person who sees through it will proceed to pursue his own advantage regardless of conventional prohibitions. It is that the stronger or superior rightly deserve to get more; their superior merit suffers injustice from the equal justice of convention.

Although we may well note that such insight into conventional justice arises from a certain philosophical position, Callicles asserts that Socrates could see the truth about these matters more clearly if he turned away from philosophy and engaged in political actions. Callicles is not simply an opponent of philosophy; indeed he claims that it must be part of the education of free young men if they are to be capable of any greatness or liberality (and he states the case more forcefully than, for instance, most of today's remaining defenders of liberal education). But Callicles considers that the higher purposes of mature human life are to be achieved through public action that wins reputation.

After magnifying the importance of this discussion through proclaiming Callicles' wisdom or sound education, goodwill, and frankness, Socrates first refutes him by taking *kreittōn* (stronger / superior, see note at 482b) in its sense of greater strength and engaging in some fast footwork (as Callicles has accused him earlier of doing?) regarding nature and law. Asked by Socrates whether the many are not by nature stronger than the few, Callicles agrees. (He does not think to object, as a contract theorist like Hobbes would, that the many are not *by nature* stronger but only become stronger when they unite through convention, contract, law.) Therefore, Socrates infers, the egalitarian justice held by the many is in fact imposed by the stronger and hence is in accordance with the justice of nature to which Callicles adheres.

Callicles, more irked than persuaded by that refutation, makes clear that by "stronger" he means "superior," not just endowed with greater bodily strength. His insistence on that point reflects the seriousness and the noble aspiration that are prominent aspects of his character. The greatest weakness associated with his position is that, though perhaps he divines, he cannot yet clearly and coherently articulate in what superiority consists (nor exactly what the superior should have more of). Socrates then leads the discussion toward superiority that rests on knowledge (a line of argument that, allowed to develop, could well issue in a notion of rulers in the precise sense such as Socrates elaborates in discussion with Thrasymachus in the *Republic*). Callicles, however, rejects Socrates' examples of knowledge as trivial and irrelevant.

Restating what he means by superior, Callicles emphasizes once more that the arena of superiority and entitlement that he has in mind is the realm of political rule, and he adds courage to intelligence as crucial aspects of the superior. With justice for the intelligent and courageous the subject of discussion, Socrates next inquires, naturally enough, into these rulers' self-rule or moderation. Here Callicles shows that his rejection of conventional opinions involves not justice alone but also moderation; with restated emphasis on his outspokenness, he launches a contemptuous attack on the moderation favored by common opinion as part and parcel of the whole delusion and swindle of conventional egalitarian justice. He extols the unrestrained satisfaction of desires, an intemperate hedonism. Is such pleasure-seeking what Callicles really aims at in his life, or do his statements here reflect his resistance to being guided by common opinions together with an incapacity to articulate the nobler and more demanding goals to which he is nonetheless somehow drawn? Inclining toward the latter alternative, I believe that Callicles is embarrassed by the examples of shameful pleasures that Socrates proceeds to elaborate but nevertheless sticks to his guns out of a certain sense of what manliness in argument requires.

However that may be, Socrates can and does here transform his argumentative task from the more difficult defense of justice to the easier argument in favor of moderation. Callicles' character and the consequently contentious conversational context make even that task hard enough, and (as noted already in the general introduction) Socrates tests a variety of rhetorical approaches: a couple of mythical (or mystical) images of the soul, a reduction to the shameful, and then other dialectical arguments— which Callicles refuses to carry through to their end until prevailed upon by Gorgias to do so. A contrast with the Polus section of the dialogue is notable: there Socrates criticizes Polus's several rhetorical approaches, insisting on his own dialectical argumentation alone; here Socrates himself tries several means of persuasion on Callicles.

Callicles does at last abandon his defense of untrammeled hedonism, though in a manner that calls his frankness in the discussion into question. In developing the rest of his arguments, Socrates treats justice and moderation (and sometimes piety too) as interchangeable (or as harmonious parts of the larger whole of human well-being) and on that basis reestablishes the distinction between flattering pursuits that provide pleasures of whatever sort and genuinely artful pursuits that aim at the good. Flute playing, choral singing, and tragedy seek to provide pleasure not good; tragedy in particular, stripped of rhythm and harmony, is rhetoric that purveys pleasure to large mixed audiences of men, women, and children, free and slave. Political rhetoric, according to Callicles, is of two kinds: one that merely flatters and another that aims at the citizens' genuine good; the latter he considers exemplified by founders and upholders of Athenian empire like Themistocles and Pericles. Elaborating what a true art of rhetoric or politics would be, Socrates shows that it would not indulge desires but would withhold such indulgence from, and so chastise, souls that are not altogether healthy. At this point Callicles rebels once again, refusing to continue, perhaps because the argument here puts Socrates in a hectoring role, an overseeing position of superiority to Callicles that the latter's love of freedom and sense of manly independence cannot accept.

Callicles describes Socrates' desire to complete this argument as violent, and urges him to find some other interlocutor; none forthcoming, Callicles suggests that Socrates complete it by himself. When Socrates questions whether the opinion of those present favors finishing the argument, it is

Gorgias who expresses his wish for it to be completed. Socrates invites objections to his account, because, he says, he does not have knowledge but is seeking in common with them (506a). Socrates' account culminates in a kind of rhetoric of geometry: a vision of heaven and earth, human beings and gods, bound together in an orderly manner by geometrical proportion and harmony. Callicles' error regarding moderation and justice is traced to his lack of care for geometry. Despite the apparent strength of Socrates' assertions about justice, moderation, and knowledge, he nonetheless again disclaims knowledge even as he describes his arguments as iron and adamantine: "I do not know how these things are, but of those people I fall in with, as now, no one who says something different is able not to be ridiculous" (509a). These Socratic disclaimers of knowledge invite comparison with aspects of the earlier discussions with Polus and Gorgias. Socrates earlier rejected Polus's rhetorical turn of laughing down an argument, but here he apparently invokes his own dialectical variant of rejection by ridicule. More importantly, in discussing rhetoric with Gorgias, Socrates descanted on how the rhetorician persuades without knowing, unlike the teacher whose didactic persuasion is the communication of his knowledge; but as nonknower, Socrates likewise persuades (when he succeeds in persuading) without knowledge (and so denies, for instance in the *Apology*, that he is a teacher, somewhat as Gorgias according to Meno denies that he teaches virtue). Socratic dialectic has more in common with rhetoric than first meets the eye.

Addressing Callicles' reproach that he cannot adequately help himself or his friends, Socrates reasonably concedes (to Callicles' warm approval) that one would wish for the power and capacity to defend oneself from suffering injustice. But—contrary to the universalist aspect of Gorgias's claim for his rhetoric—Socrates argues that such power is relative to the political regime; one must become like the regime in order to have political power in it. And if the regime is unjust, one must then become unjust to avoid suffering injustice; that is, one would erroneously choose the greater evil of corrupting one's soul so as to defend against the lesser evil of suffering some injustice.

Callicles cannot accept that position, against which he restates that the man with power akin to the regime will kill the one without such power and confiscate his property. Conceding the point, Socrates responds that it will be a base man killing a noble and good one. Just this, Callicles exclaims, is what he finds infuriating. Socrates dismisses that reaction as irrational: Callicles might just as well honor each and every life-preserving art or practice, whether swimming or navigation or military engineering; but Callicles considers himself clearly superior to these practitioners. Rather than be concerned with the preservation of life, a good man leaves such matters to the gods, accepts the typical women's view of destiny, and strives for the best life. Socrates concludes this section of his argument by repeating that no art can give one great power in the city while being unlike the regime. "For you must be not an imitator but like these men in your very own nature, if you are to achieve something genuine in friendship with the Athenian people" (513b).

Callicles states a mixed and murky reaction to Socrates' account: "In some way, I don't know what, what you say seems good to me, Socrates; but I suffer the experience of the many—I am not altogether persuaded by you." Socrates attributes Callicles' recalcitrance to that same love of the people that he had identified in Callicles at the start of their discussion, but suggests that frequent recurrence to these and similar arguments might persuade Callicles in the longer run. (In case of Socrates' unavailability, soon to be foreshadowed by his frank recognition of the dangers he faces from unjust accusers in Athens, could written arguments do the job?) Callicles, it seems, does love the people, and this condition would seem to favor his capacity to gain political power in democratic Athens. The cost of such power in the terms Socrates has been using in this context would be to become unjust like the many; Callicles perhaps feels it as a loss of the superiority to the many that he claims. Though not wholly persuaded, Callicles does have some openness to Socrates' argument, perhaps because Callicles in a sense loves the people but also holds himself decidedly superior to the many; and whereas his own attempts to articulate the nature of such superiority keep falling short, flat, or apart, Socrates holds forth some as yet dimly perceived grounds of real superiority.

Socrates gives some elaboration of what a true rhetorical art or a true political art would do: rejecting the goal of satisfying desires and providing pleasures, it would make the citizens as good as possible. With that criterion in mind, Socrates considers the four examples of good political rhetoric and statesmanship that Callicles had mentioned earlier and finds them all wanting. If Pericles, for instance, had had a true political rhetorical art, he would have made the citizens more just, which means tamer and less savage, but in fact the people turned against him after he had led them for many years. Hence, on the implicit premise that an art has all the power it needs to attain its end, Socrates concludes that Pericles lacked that art. Responding to Callicles' reassertion that the statesmen of Athens' past are superior to those of the present, Socrates makes clear his fundamental critique of Athenian imperialism, which he compares to stuffing someone with an excess of pleasant foods; he warns that the originators of such practices are falsely honored, whereas those present when the ultimate badness becomes manifest—perhaps Callicles and Alcibiades—end up taking the blame.

Against Socrates' depiction of a true art of politics that fights, against the people's desires, for the sake of their true good, Callicles admits that the kind of politics he plans to practice is one that serves the people or, as Socrates calls it, flatters them. When Callicles is about to say once again that without such deeds of flattery one would be at the mercy of one's enemies, Socrates cuts him off. At this point Callicles expresses his judgment that Socrates, relying on living out of the way, does not really believe that he could indeed be the victim of such unjust harm. Socrates emphatically denies any such false belief. He suggests that he does in fact practice the true political art, opposing people's desires and pleasures so as to aim solely at their genuine good. Accordingly, Socrates says, if he were unjustly accused before the multitude, he would have nothing to say; he would be like a doctor (who uses bitter medicine, dieting, and surgery) accused by a pastry cook before a jury of children. His true defense, that he did these things for the people's good, would not persuade effectively. Thus here Socrates takes the view that the true political or rhetorical art altogether lacks the power to achieve its end.

To Callicles' sensible question whether this is not a bad situation to be in, Socrates once more repeats that the important thing is not to avoid suffering but to avoid doing injustice. He adds that a good man should not fear death or suffering any other injustice, but only arriving at Hades with his soul disfigured by deeds of injustice. The discussion ends with an extensive depiction of the soul's fate in Hades: Socrates supposes that the sophisticated Callicles will take it as myth, though Socrates himself calls it an account or argument (*logos*). Here divine judgment and divinely administered punishments are said to accomplish what he earlier attributed to justice as part of the art of politics: healing men's souls, through painful means. We are gently reminded of the difficulty of that task by being told that the job of judging was once upon a time rather poorly performed, before certain improvements were instituted by Zeus. How much worse must actual justice administered by human beings be! And we are left with the terrifying possibility that some souls may be incurable even by divine means. Such souls are then simply punished painfully for all eternity as a lesson for those who arrive in Hades. We cannot know whether Callicles is much affected by this conclusion.

The final part of Socrates' discussion with Callicles is thus strongly marked by stark, extreme formulations. A true art of politics pursues good only, not pleasure; what is pleasant can be the subject of no art. The good man cares nothing for preservation and only for the best life possible. A true art of politics has all the power it needs, and therefore Pericles must not have had it; the true art of politics as practiced by Socrates pursues good only and nothing pleasant, therefore Socrates would have no power to defend himself from unjust accusation. These and other similar formulations lead some to believe that the *Gorgias* reveals Plato at his most moralistic and most bitter against Athens in particular or politics in general. Maybe so, but perhaps a distinctively Socratic philosophical rhetoric is involved here. No one formulation is the whole truth. Socrates' extreme formulations are not the whole story but are instead what most needs emphasis in the particular context of the discussion, for instance what the interlocutor most needs to hear in order to correct his own characteristic errors or vices. Surely Socrates' formulations succeeded in engaging the attention of Gorgias; perhaps too they are meant to suggest certain topics, useful for Gorgias and beneficial to the political community, that Gorgias could do a better job of presenting rhetorically than Socrates.

To recapitulate: in the discussion with Gorgias, Socrates brings to light Gorgias's overstated claim for the power of rhetoric and reveals the tensions or contradictions within Gorgias's position, between public concerns and private goals. In the Polus section Socrates demonstrates the consequences of Gorgias's failure to take public goals, or the teaching of justice, seriously. Polus dangerously announces what Gorgias tried to deal with indirectly and discretely: the conflict between rhetoric and public standards of justice. Polus's praise of successful injustice makes explicit that private goals have priority in his own thinking; but his anger points toward the possibility of a more public vocation. Socrates succeeds in refuting this young intellectual and perhaps begins to turn his eagerness and anger toward the defense of justice. With Callicles, who aspires to act as a statesman in his native Athens, Socrates exhibits the limitations of his power of persuasion: Callicles would not even have permitted the argument to come to a conclusion had not Gorgias intervened. Callicles' conception of a natural right of the stronger or superior to rule suggests a possible merging of private ambition with public function, but this is impossible under the influence of the Pindaric or Sophistic conception of justice, which forces

Callicles, though deeply moved by some conception of superiority or nobility, to think of the end as private pleasure. Socrates can refute but not persuade him. Genuine persuasion, Socrates seems to suggest, would need to rest on a complete vision of order and proportion in this world, in our relation to the gods, and in our fate after death. Because Gorgias, unlike Socrates, can speak to the many, one wonders whether he might not present such a vision more persuasively to many than Socrates. And because this dialogue also presents the likely inferiority of the students or followers to the great innovators, one is led to reflect on the possible value, perhaps the indispensable role, that writings might have for the success of any long-term effort of persuasion along the suggested lines. The issues of rhetoric and writing, of course, direct us toward the *Phaedrus*.